PIZZA LOVER'S
COOKBOOK

PIZZA LOVER'S COOKBOOK

Creative and Delicious Recipes for
Making the World's Favorite Food

GREGORY D. BOOCK & KIRK S. STUART

PRIMA PUBLISHING

PRIMA PUBLISHING and colophon are registered trademarks of Prima Communications, Inc.

Library of Congress Cataloging-in-Publication Data

Boock, Gregory D.
    Pizza lover's cookbook : creative and delicious recipes for making the world's favorite food / by Gregory D. Boock and Kirk S. Stuart.
        p.   cm.
    Reprint. Originally published under title: Gourmet pizzas. Simon and Schuster, 1995.
    Includes index.
    ISBN 0-7615-0448-6
    1. Pizza.   I. Stuart, Kirk S.   II. Boock, Gregory D. Gourmet pizzas.
III. Title.
TX770.P58B66   1996
641.8'24—dc20   96-22971
                                                              CIP

96 97 98 99 00 01 AA 10 9 8 7 6 5 4 3 2

Printed in the United States of America

How to Order:
Single copies may be ordered from Prima Publishing, P.O. Box 1260BK, Rocklin, CA 95677; telephone (916) 632-4400. Quantity discounts are also available. On your letterhead, include information concerning the intended use of the books and the number of books you wish to purchase.

Visit us online at http://www.primapublishing.com

Contents

〜〜〜

Acknowledgments

~~~

I WOULD LIKE TO ACKNOWLEDGE THE ASSISTANCE OF BUTTERFIELDS
CHEESE FACTORS, WHO PROVIDED TECHNICAL SPECIFICATIONS ON ALL
THE CHEESES USED THROUGHOUT THE BOOK.

THANKS ARE ALSO DUE TO MY VEGETABLE PROVIDER, LEO,
AT NORTHPOINT FRUIT, FOR THE ONGOING SUPPLY OF EXCELLENT
PRODUCE, AT ANY TIME OF THE DAY, FOR THE PHOTOGRAPHIC SHOOT
(EVEN IF WE DIDN'T USE IT IN THE FINAL SHOTS!).

AND THANK YOU TO THE EXCEPTIONALLY PATIENT AND CREATIVE
FOOD STYLISTS, MEGAN AND SIOBHAN; THE PHOTOGRAPHER, STEPHEN;
AND MY EDITOR, SIOBHAN.

LAST, AND CERTAINLY NOT LEAST, THANK YOU TO MY MUM, PATRICIA, FOR
TREMENDOUS DEDICATION AND LOVE THROUGHOUT MY LIFE.

THE PUBLISHER WOULD LIKE TO THANK GEORGINA DOLLING
PRODUCTIONS AND HOME & GARDEN ON THE MALL, SYDNEY, FOR THEIR
GENEROSITY IN SUPPLYING PROPS FOR PHOTOGRAPHY.

Introduction

~~~

History traces the origin of the pizza back to the Persian empire of 500 BC, when the Roman soldiers made camp bread containing locally available fruits and nuts. It is speculated that this style of bread bore a resemblance to what we now know as pizza.

It wasn't until the 1700s that peasant families in Naples, Italy, first began using tomatoes as a part of the topping. In fact, it was a local baker or *pizzaiolo,* Don Raffaele Esposito, who developed the infamous margherita combination in honor of the Queen's birthday. Using the colors of the flag for inspiration, he made a pizza with mozzarella, tomato, and fresh basil.

Italian immigrants soon took the pizza to North America in the late 1800s and the first pizzeria was established in New York City in 1895. The pizza continued to snowball in popularity and it soon became a national, and then global, food item.

In the late 1980s, people became more aware of fats and cholesterol, and learned how to count calories. The results saw some inspiring chefs, such as Wolfgang Puck, reinterpret the modern pizza, making it a culinary delight by using exotic ingredients and cooking the pizzas in wood-fired ovens. With a very fast cooking time and using minimal amounts of oil, the ingredients maintained their freshness, vitamin counts remained high, and the fat content stayed low. The gourmet pizza was born!

This new style of pizza received favorable reaction from all types of pizza connoisseurs: the young, the middle-aged, and the elderly. Indeed, the gourmet pizza stretches across the generation gap and, with its mass market appeal, will remain as one of the staple foods within our society. So long as there are people willing to create and sample new produce, or reinvent the old, the pizza will retain its popularity.

The Basics

THE BASIC EQUIPMENT

STONEWARE

At the restaurant, we use specially imported pizza ovens to achieve a crisp, golden pizza base. These ovens run at a much higher temperature than your average domestic oven. The best way to achieve a similar result at home is to cook your pizza on an unglazed terracotta tile.

A hand-molded tile about 12 inches square and approximately ¾ inch thick is ideal. These molded tiles retain the heat better than factory-extruded ones. They are fairly inexpensive and are available from terracotta studios or tiling stores.

METALWARE

PIZZA PADDLE: An extremely handy piece of equipment, a pizza paddle or baker's peel is basically an oversized spatula. It is about 10 inches square, with a bevelled edge to allow you to slip the paddle under your pizza and lift it into the oven with no mess or fuss, and, most importantly, in one piece! A gentle push and the pizza slides off onto the cooking tile.

When the pizza is done, the paddle will easily slide under it and retrieve it from the stoneware on which it was baked. Alternatively, a pair of wide spatulas will do the job, but not as safely as a paddle.

PIZZA CUTTER: I highly recommend using a pizza cutter or wheel to slice your pizza, but don't try and race through the pizza as you may end up with a big mess and all the topping dragged from one side to the other. With some of the dessert pizzas that appear later in the book, it is safest to cut them with a large chopping or cook's knife. This helps to keep the ingredients in place and makes the presentation a lot better.

FOOD PROCESSOR OR MIXER: There are number of good food processors on the market, so shop around for one that will easily accommodate a batch of pizza dough. If you don't have a food processor, there is no need to worry as I have included a method using the good, old-fashioned rolling pin; it will just take a little bit longer and require a little more effort.

HARDWARE

SCALES: Scales are a necessary tool for any successful baking. It is essential that they are accurate, especially when dealing with yeast.

GENERAL

The following general equipment will also be needed when making your pizzas:

- a good selection of mixing bowls
- a large wire whisk
- a measuring cup
- a chopping board
- saucepans
- a frying pan or skillet
- roasting trays

THE BASIC INGREDIENTS

~~~

FLOUR

Basically, three varieties of flour are used throughout this book. All are readily available from your supermarket.

ALL-PURPOSE FLOUR: This flour is of medium protein or gluten content. Gluten is what gives flour its strength and structure when used in dough products. Any commercially available flour is suitable.

WHOLE WHEAT FLOUR: Unlike all-purpose flour, this flour still contains the wheat germ. This means it is higher in fiber and nutrition. Use one of the brands readily available from your supermarket.

SEMOLINA: This flour is made from crushing a cereal, usually hard wheat, into granules.

Semolina that has been medium to finely ground is required. Once your pizza dough has been rolled out to shape, the board is sprinkled with semolina and the dough placed on top. This stops the pizza base from sticking to the board and, when you are ready to place it into the oven, it will slide off easily. You will not need a great deal of this flour. It lasts indefinitely, so simply buy a small bag and store in an airtight container until needed.

YEAST

Yeast is a minute form of plant life that belongs to the fungi family and can multiply rapidly under ideal conditions.

ACTIVE DRY YEAST: A high-activity yeast that is dried and vacuum-packed to preserve its freshness and life. It is conveniently packaged in small envelopes and will remain active for at least two years. This is the yeast with which we will be dealing. It is readily available from your supermarket.

COMPRESSED FRESH YEAST: The fresh or compressed yeast that is sold in larger quantities reacts more quickly in dough-making, but it has a short shelf life and is generally available only to commercial kitchens.

OLIVE OIL

The secret to producing the desired crispy crust for your pizza lies in the oil content of your dough: the oil provides an improved heat transfer between the crust and the baking surface, as well as imparting wonderful flavor to the dough.

PURE: This is essentially the second grade of olive oil. It has a mild olive taste and is fairly cheap to use, but it may have a cloudy look to it.

EXTRA-VIRGIN: This is the among the top lines of olive oil. As its name suggests, it comes from the first pressing of the olive and is stronger in taste and flavor than pure.

TOMATO SAUCE

The tomato or pizza sauce that makes up the base of your pizza topping requires a few simple considerations to be taken into account: how sweet it should be, how herbaceous, and what consistency to make it. It took eight months of testing and development to arrive at the tomato sauce we use at The Red Centre restaurant, and this recipe is given later on in the book.

In season, fresh tomatoes are wonderful to use in your base sauce. However, you will have to allow for changes in the water content of the fruit—your sauce may be too thin at some times and too thick at others. Canned crushed tomatoes are always the same consistency so they make an excellent choice for your base sauce.

CHEESE

Since the introduction of the gourmet pizza, gone are the days when the only cheese you would find on a pizza was mozzarella. At The Red Centre we use a range of eight to ten different cheeses. Below is an outline of the styles and characteristics of some of these.

MOZZARELLA: The godfather of pizza cheeses, mozzarella originated in southern Italy. It has a mild flavor and a soft, white texture, with good melting properties.

BLUE CHEESE: Choose a young, firm blue cheese with a sharp flavor, such as young Gorgonzola. Once matured, the cheese becomes much smoother, but with a bolder blue flavor.

GOAT CHEESE OR CHÈVRE: This is a very creamy and flavorful cheese with acidic properties. Each brand of goat cheese will vary in taste, so it's important that you try them and select the one you prefer. Types to choose from include Montrachet, Bucheron, and Milawa.

BRIE: Choose a rich, full-cream Brie with a sweet aftertaste, such as the French *Brie de Meaux*.

BOCCONCINI: A soft curd cheese of a mozzarella type, bocconcini is a very mild cheese, slightly acidic in flavor.

GRANA PADANO PARMESAN: This is a grainy or granulated Parmesan, intense and sharp in taste, and is aged between 14 and 18 months before being sold. It is produced in Italy. About one quarter of Italian cow's milk production is taken up in the manufacture of grana cheeses.

CHEDDAR: At the restaurant, we use Stokes Point Cheddar, a young, pleasantly smooth-flavored cheese with a lingering full flavor, an open texture, and a crumbly consistency. There is a large range of Cheddar cheeses to choose from, so shop around until you find the one that you prefer.

CURED MEATS

In this section I am simply providing my preferred choice for cured meats. The strength and flavor will vary from brand to brand, so once again shop around until you find the brand that you prefer.

PEPPERONI: This Italian salami is a pork and beef mixture that is finely minced or ground. Pepperoni is spicy and hot, with a slightly smoky flavor.

SICILIANO: A traditional coarse, chunky salami, Siciliano is highly flavored with more than a liberal sprinkling of crushed chile peppers and sweet tomato paste. This salami is very hot!

PROSCIUTTO PARMA: Whole pork legs are trimmed and aged with sea salt, then massaged by hand to expel excess moisture and aged with the bone in for 12 months to develop flavor and taste. The final product is sensational cured meat that is full of flavor, providing an excellent accompaniment to many dishes.

SEAFOOD

There are only two rules to apply to any seafood that you use: always buy the best and make sure it is fresh. When precooking seafood, be sure to cook the item until it is "just done," that is, so that the seafood is almost cooked but not quite. Bear in mind that the pizza will be going back into the oven to cook and so will any seafood that is topping it.

The time to go to the market to buy your produce is after you have decided to make a seafood pizza. You may, in fact, see other shellfish there that you would like to try.

SHRIMP: Frozen shrimp are acceptable for use on pizza toppings, but it is far better to go to the trouble of buying fresh ones. Always peel and devein them before use.

SCALLOPS: Buy fresh scallops from your local fishmonger or go to the markets to select them. You may choose to buy your scallops complete with roe to add extra flavor or, alternatively, simply use the scallop without roe.

OCTOPUS: A wonderful and interesting item to put on your pizzas, but be sure to clean the octopus properly and take care not to overcook. Select baby octopus as it looks better on the finished pizza and will not have to be trimmed as much.

MUSSELS: If the prospect of steaming open your own mussels seems a bit daunting, buy mussels that have been marinated in brine instead.

OYSTERS: Choose fresh oysters in the half shell so that you get the real flavor without the addition of salty brine. These delicate bivalves deserve to be served *au naturel*.

SMOKED SALMON: You may find salmon pieces or trimmings at the markets, which are perfect for using on a pizza. Otherwise, use sliced smoked salmon. It may be quite expensive, but you will only need about 3 ounces per pizza.

CAVIAR: For some people, the thought of caviar on a pizza may well be hard to imagine, but it is delicious when nestled on a large dollop of crème fraîche on top of smoked salmon. There is also some very good salmon roe available that is good to use. Although it is orange in color and larger in size than caviar, it provides an equally acceptable topping.

From time to time I use other seasonal seafood such as tuna, sardines, scampi, and Atlantic salmon as pizza toppings. You are really only limited by your imagination when it comes to making your own creations. Don't be afraid to experiment with new things.

WHAT'S INSTANTLY AVAILABLE?

PIZZA BASES: Much to my surprise, I was delighted to find a wide range of pizza bases for sale. They vary in size from small (about 6 inches in diameter) to large (about 10 inches). These bases are available fresh, vacuum-sealed or frozen, so you can always have some in the freezer for the times when you crave a pizza, but don't have time to make the dough.

Another alternative is to use pocket or pita breads, which make a suitable base and are available in reduced salt, yeast-free, whole wheat, and regular forms. It is really a matter of choice and finding out what you like, as some bases may be too thick, too dry, or just not quite right for some reason.

TOMATO SAUCE BASE: I have found two products on the supermarket shelves that are called "pizza sauce." These can provide a quick, tasty base sauce when you don't have enough time to make your own. You may also like to try some of the chunky-style pasta sauces that are commercially available.

PIZZA CHEESES: Mozzarella is one cheese that is abundantly available, whether it be grated or in the traditional small balls. Most of the cheeses I have already mentioned are on hand in the cheese section of good supermarkets or at delicatessens, but feel free to replace them with other favorites or to try some new ones.

THE PANTRY

Following is a collection of the base recipes that are used several times throughout this book. They should be made ahead of time, so you may need to plan ahead before diving in to make your first pizza. All sauces will last in the refrigerator for up to two weeks, some even longer, so you can keep any leftovers for your next pizza session.

BASIC PIZZA DOUGH

This recipe makes eight dough balls. Any excess dough can be stored in the freezer until required.

STARTER

4 scant tablespoons active dry yeast

5 teaspoons granulated sugar

⅔ cup lukewarm or room-temperature water (the water temperature should not exceed 98°F)

2 cups all-purpose flour

DOUGH

¼ cup olive oil

1¾ cups lukewarm or room-temperature water

2 teaspoons salt

6 cups all-purpose flour

MAKES 8 DOUGH BALLS

STARTER

Combine the yeast and sugar with the water in a small bowl. Whisk together to incorporate. Pour into the mixing bowl of a food processor. Add the flour and pulse (using an on/off action) to mix.

DOUGH

Pour the olive oil into the water. Mix the salt into the flour and add to the starter dough in the food processor (fitted with a metal blade). Add the oil/water mixture. Pulse until a ball starts to form, 1–2 minutes should be sufficient. You should now have a nice, smooth dough.

Remove the dough from the processor and dust lightly with flour to absorb any excess moisture. Place in a lightly floured bowl and cover with a damp cloth. Leave to rise in a warm place until the dough has doubled in size, about 30 minutes. If you are not going to use the dough immediately, place in the refrigerator. This will slow down the rising process and prevent the dough from growing too much in size.

Punch down the dough. This process is where the dough is smacked to release any gases that may have built up during rising. Roll the dough back into a ball and divide into 8 pieces (about 8 ounces each). Roll each piece into a ball, then wrap each one in plastic wrap and return to the refrigerator until you are ready to use for the pizza base. If you are not going to use the dough immediately, store in the freezer until needed.

When you want to make your pizza, remove the dough ball from the refrigerator and allow to stand until it reaches room temperature. This will make the dough easier to stretch and roll out.

WHOLE WHEAT PIZZA DOUGH

~~~

Although this is a whole wheat dough recipe, only a third of the flour is whole wheat because the all-purpose flour makes the dough lighter and easier to handle.

STARTER

4 scant tablespoons active dry yeast
5 teaspoons granulated sugar
⅔ cup lukewarm or room-temperature water (the water temperature should not exceed 98°F)
2 cups all-purpose flour

DOUGH

¼ cup olive oil
1¾ cups lukewarm or room-temperature water
2 teaspoons salt
4 cups all-purpose flour
2 cups whole wheat flour

MAKES 8 DOUGH BALLS

The method for whole wheat pizza dough is the same as for the basic dough (see opposite).

TO MAKE THE DOUGH BY HAND

Combine the dry ingredients in a large bowl and make a well in the center. Pour the liquid ingredients in the well and gradually incorporate the dry ingredients from around the sides of the bowl. Once the ingredients are combined, remove from the bowl and knead the dough vigorously on a floured surface for 5–10 minutes or until the dough is smooth.

Transfer to a large bowl lightly dusted with flour and cover with a damp cloth. Leave the dough to rise in a warm place until it has doubled in size, about 30 minutes. Once again, if you are not going to use the dough right away, place it in the refrigerator and allow to rise over several hours instead. Continue as for processor dough (see opposite).

HOW TO ROLL YOUR DOUGH

Clear some space on your work bench or counter. You will remember that I spoke about semolina earlier in this chapter; well, this is where you use it. Lightly sprinkle both the bench and your dough ball with semolina. Take the dough ball and flatten it out using the palms of your hands, then place it on the bench to begin rolling.

Start gently working the dough with a rolling pin. Give it several rolls back and forth to make it egg-shaped as you face it, and then turn it around 90 degrees, so that the egg shape is horizontal to you. Sprinkle some more semolina over the dough if it is starting to stick. Continue rolling the dough in each direction until it becomes round and approximately 10 inches in diameter, or the size of a medium pizza.

Take a flat tray with no edges (such as a baking sheet) and sprinkle it liberally with semolina. This is what you will make your pizza on. Place the pizza base onto the tray and let the dough relax or rest for 5 minutes. (This is the ideal time to roll out another base.) You are now ready to top your pizza.

PIZZA SAUCE
〰️

The quantities below will make enough tomato sauce for approximately six pizzas.

2 teaspoons olive oil
5 ounces onions, diced
1 teaspoon crushed garlic
8 basil leaves, freshly chopped
4 teaspoons tomato paste
1⅔ cups (14 ounces) crushed tomatoes

MAKES APPROXIMATELY 2 CUPS

Heat the olive oil in a medium saucepan over a medium heat. Add the onion and garlic. Sauté for 3–5 minutes until the onion is transparent. Add the remaining ingredients and bring to the boil. Remove from the heat and blend or process the mixture into a purée. Allow to cool. Store in an airtight container in the refrigerator until ready to use.

PESTO SAUCE

~~~~

A thick, fragrant sauce made from olive oil, basil, and garlic which has a multitude of uses, its robust flavor enhances and complements many a pizza at our restaurant. This pesto will last indefinitely if stored in the refrigerator, so make a batch and you'll have it on hand whenever the urge strikes you. This pesto is cooked and will therefore last longer than uncooked varieties, especially as it does not contain Parmesan cheese.

1 cup olive oil
1 large yellow onion, diced
⅓ cup pine nuts
8 cloves garlic, crushed
3 large handfuls of fresh basil leaves
salt and freshly ground black pepper,
   to taste

MAKES APPROXIMATELY 2 CUPS

Heat half of the olive oil in a medium saucepan over a medium heat. Add the onion, pine nuts, and garlic. Cook, stirring continuously, until the pine nuts start to turn golden (be careful, as they will quickly scorch). Add the basil and the remainder of the oil. Simmer the mixture for 3–5 minutes, then remove from the heat.

   Place the mixture in an electric blender or food processor. Blend or process until smooth, then season with salt and pepper. Store in an airtight container in the refrigerator until ready to use.

BARBECUE SAUCE

~~~~

If you feel up to making your own barbecue sauce, here's a recipe for one. It can be used as the base sauce when making your pizzas.

4 teaspoons olive oil
2 medium red onions, diced
1 teaspoon crushed garlic
1⅗ cups (13 fl ounces) ketchup
⅓ cup Worcestershire sauce
2 tablespoons cider vinegar
1 teaspoon Dijon mustard
8 teaspoons brown sugar
4 teaspoons chili powder
4 teaspoons paprika
¼ teaspoon cayenne or red pepper
¼ teaspoon ground coriander
¼ teaspoon ground cumin
1 teaspoon liquid smoke (available from
   good delicatessens or Tex Mex supply
   stores)

MAKES APPROXIMATELY 3 CUPS

Heat the olive oil in a saucepan over a medium heat. Add the onion and garlic; sauté until they are transparent. Add the remaining ingredients and reduce the heat to low. Simmer uncovered for 15 minutes, stirring occasionally. Store the sauce in an airtight container in the refrigerator until ready to use.

ROAST VEGETABLES

~~~~~

The most common roast vegetables used in the creation of our pizzas include tomatoes, bell peppers, and onions. Here are basic methods for preparing each item.

ROAST TOMATOES

Use the small- to medium-size Roma or plum tomatoes. To prepare for roasting, simply cut in half lengthways and lay face up on a roasting pan. Season with salt and freshly ground black pepper. Bake at 275°F for 30–40 minutes or until the tomatoes appear dried out and reduced in size.

What you are doing here is removing the water from within the tomatoes and concentrating the juice, making it tastier and sweeter. If you wish, you can take the drying process further and completely dry out the tomatoes to make your own "oven-dried" tomatoes. These can be stored in jars in canola or olive oil.

For a typical pizza, you will need about 4–6 whole tomatoes.

ROAST ONIONS

The red Spanish onions are best for this as they add a wonderful color to the pizza, along with a much milder taste than yellow or white onions. Size isn't important when selecting your onions as they are cut into wedges before roasting.

Prepare three to four onions at a time. Peel the onions and cut lengthwise into wedges no wider than 1 inch. Place in a roasting pan with a little olive or vegetable oil. Season with salt and freshly ground black pepper.

Roast at 325°F for 10 minutes. Stir the onions and place back in the oven for another 10 minutes. Remove from the oven and allow to cool. Drain any water off the onions and set them aside until ready to use. If they are going into the refrigerator, cover them with plastic wrap or store in an airtight container.

ROAST BELL PEPPERS

Roasting this vegetable develops the inbred sweetness of bell peppers. Once roasted, peeled, and cleaned, the bell pepper is easily cut into a diverse range of shapes to garnish the top of your pizza.

To roast bell peppers, place them on a roasting tray in the oven at 475°F. Roast until their skins are evenly blistered and browned, about 20 minutes, turning them two or three times during cooking to color evenly.

Remove from the oven and place into a metal bowl. Cover the bowl with plastic wrap. The heat from the peppers will create steam and this will help to loosen the charred skin.

When cool enough to handle, simply pull the stems out of the peppers and wash the skin off under cold, running water. Remove any seeds or membrane, and cut the flesh into strips or diamonds or triangles, or whatever shape takes your fancy.

ROAST GARLIC

To do this successfully, it is better to roast several heads of garlic at the same time. The resulting garlic purée will keep for some time in an airtight container in the refrigerator.

As the garlic roasts, its pungent acids are lost and the natural sugars in it begin to caramelize, so the garlic becomes sweeter and it loses that sometimes offensive aftertaste.

Place several heads of garlic in a small roasting pan and coat with oil. Roast in the oven at 300°F for 1–2 hours or until the garlic is soft and mushy. Remove from the oven and allow to cool.

Drain off any oil and set aside. Cut the roots off the garlic and squeeze the pulp into a bowl. Discard the garlic "shell." Add the reserved oil to the pulp and combine thoroughly. The garlic purée is now ready to use.

SOME IMPORTANT COOKING TIPS

The following tips are most important for the successful baking of your pizzas. If you keep them in mind every time you bake a gourmet pizza, or any pizza for that matter, you should not go far wrong.

- When topping your pizza base, always keep a 1¼ inch border around the edge of the base clean. Not only will your pizza look better when cooked, this also means that the topping will not ooze over the edges and stick to your pizza stone or tile.

- Always heat your pizza stones or tiles as you preheat the oven, i.e. before you put the pizza in to bake on them. This means the dough will be crisp and golden when baked, rather than soggy.

- Experiment with your oven temperature until you find the right setting. When cooking your first pizza, preheat the oven to the highest temperature setting possible (500°F). It may be a good idea to turn the temperature down slightly when you put the pizza in to bake. Once you have cooked a few pizzas, you will be able to gauge exactly how hot your pizza stones or tiles become, and adjust your oven temperature accordingly.

- Use a pizza paddle or a wide spatula to place your pizza in the oven. This way the pizza can be gently slid onto the stone or tile, and you are less likely to upset the topping.

- The pizza base may puff up during cooking. If it does, simply prick the bubbles with a fork.

- When removing the pizza from the oven, you may find it easier to slide the pizza out onto a flat tray and then transfer it to a board for cutting. This will help to prevent cracking of the crust and any possible mishaps before you actually get your pizza to the table.

POULTRY
with a Difference

WHETHER IT'S TURKEY, DUCK OR SIMPLY CHICKEN,
THE SAME BASIC RULES APPLY.

THE BREAST FILLETS WILL ALWAYS YIELD THE A-GRADE
MEAT, BUT THEY WON'T NECESSARILY HAVE THE BEST
FLAVOR. THE THIGH AND DRUMSTICK ARE USUALLY A
DARKER, MORE FLAVORFUL CUT. IT REQUIRES SOME
SKILL TO REMOVE THE BONES, SO ASK YOUR BUTCHER
TO DO THIS FOR YOU IF YOU CAN'T FIND THIGHS
ALREADY BONED AT YOUR SUPERMARKET.

ALWAYS METICULOUSLY REMOVE ANY SINEW, SKIN, OR FAT
FROM THE POULTRY BEFORE USING IT. WHEN MARINATING
POULTRY, A FEW INCISIONS CUT INTO THE MEAT WILL
ALLOW THE MARINADE TO BE ABSORBED MORE QUICKLY.

FINALLY, NEVER OVERCOOK POULTRY AS IT WILL
BECOME DRY AND STRINGY.

Tandoori Chicken

~~~

THIS PIZZA REQUIRES A FAIR BIT OF GROUNDWORK BEFORE IT CAN BE MADE,
BUT THE RESULTS ARE WELL WORTH THE PREPARATION TIME INVOLVED.
IT IS GARNISHED WITH MANGO RELISH AND CUCUMBER YOGURT. IF ANY
RELISH OR YOGURT IS LEFT OVER, THEY ALSO MAKE EXCELLENT
DIPS OR GARNISHES FOR COLD CUTS.

CUCUMBER YOGURT
½ cucumber, peeled, seeded, and diced
1 tablespoon chopped fresh dill
1 tablespoon chopped fresh mint
1 cup plain yogurt
salt and freshly ground black pepper,
   to taste

MANGO RELISH
1 tablespoon olive oil
1 medium onion, finely diced
scant ½ cup cider vinegar
¼ cup granulated sugar
1 mango, peeled and roughly chopped
1 cup dried apple
4 teaspoons golden raisins
4 teaspoons currants

TANDOORI PIZZA
4 teaspoons commercially prepared
   tandoori paste
scant ½ cup plain yogurt
13 ounces chicken breast, trimmed of any
   fat and sinew

salt and freshly ground black pepper,
   to taste
2 (8-ounce) dough balls (see page 8)
⅔ cup Pizza Sauce (see page 10)
1¼ cups grated mozzarella cheese
⅓ cup raw cashews, roughly chopped
½ small red onion, sliced and separated
   into rings
freshly ground black pepper (optional)
chives, chopped (optional)

MAKES 2 MEDIUM PIZZAS

CUCUMBER YOGURT
Place the cucumber in a bowl and add the
remaining ingredients. Mix well and season
with salt and pepper. Set aside until ready to
use. (Any leftover garnish can be stored in
an airtight container in the refrigerator.)

MANGO RELISH
Heat the olive oil in a medium saucepan
over a moderate heat. Add the onion and

sauté for 3 minutes or until the onion becomes transparent. Add the cider vinegar, sugar, and half of the mango pulp. (Store remainder.) Cook gently until the liquid has reduced in volume by half. Add the dried apple, golden raisins, and currants. Bring to the boil once again and simmer gently until the mixture has thickened, about 5 minutes. Remove from the heat and set aside until ready to use.

This relish can be made when mangoes are in season and will keep in the refrigerator indefinitely. This means you can make several batches when mangoes are at their cheapest and store the relish until needed. Frozen or canned mango slices are also suitable.

TANDOORI PIZZA

Whisk the tandoori paste and yogurt together until the mixture is smooth and free of lumps. Place the chicken breasts in a bowl and add enough of the tandoori sauce to coat the chicken. Leave to marinate in the refrigerator for several hours or overnight.

Preheat the oven to 350°F. Place the marinated chicken on a lightly oiled baking sheet. Bake in the oven for 15 minutes or until cooked. Allow the chicken to cool completely before cutting across the breast into very thin slices.

Place the chicken slices in a bowl and add just enough of the remaining tandoori sauce to moisten the chicken. Season with salt and pepper.

Place two pizza stones or tiles in the oven. Heat the oven to 500°F. Roll out the pizza dough, as described on page 10, so that you have two bases. Cover the bases with the Pizza Sauce and mozzarella cheese, keeping a 1¼-inch border around the edge of the dough clean.

Dot the tandoori chicken on the bases in a random pattern, leaving spaces for the other ingredients to fall into. Sprinkle with the cashews. Place the onion rings all over the top.

Using a wide spatula or pizza paddle, gently slide each pizza onto a stone or tile. Cook for 10 minutes. Remove the pizzas from the oven when cooked and golden. Season with the black pepper and garnish with some chives (if using). Slice each pizza into eight pieces and serve immediately, accompanied by the Cucumber Yogurt and Mango Relish.

Balmy Chicken with Papaya & Mango Salsa

〜〜〜

ACCOMPANIED BY A FRAGRANT AND TASTY SALSA, THIS PIZZA
IS A TROPICAL BLEND COUPLED WITH SCALLIONS,
SMOKED CHICKEN, AND BROCCOLI.

2 (8-ounce) dough balls (see page 8)
⅔ cup Pizza Sauce (see page 10)
1¼ cups grated mozzarella cheese
11 ounces smoked chicken, shredded
3 scallions, sliced on the angle, Chinese
   style
5 ounces bocconcini cheese, diced
2 heads of broccoli, cut into florets and
   blanched until almost cooked (about
   3 minutes)

PAPAYA AND MANGO SALSA

1 papaya, peeled and diced
1 mango, peeled and diced
½ red onion, peeled and diced
½ lime, peeled, segmented, and diced
¼ bunch of coriander (cilantro), finely
   chopped
¼ teaspoon chile paste, or to taste

MAKES 2 MEDIUM PIZZAS

Place two pizza stones or tiles in the oven.
Heat the oven to 500°F. Roll out the pizza
dough, as described on page 10, so that
you have two bases. Cover the bases with
the Pizza Sauce and mozzarella cheese,
keeping a 1¼-inch border around the edge
of the dough clean.

Place the smoked chicken in a random
pattern on the bases, leaving spaces for
other ingredients to fall into. Add the scallions and bocconcini cheese. Top with the
broccoli.

Using a wide spatula or pizza paddle,
gently slide each pizza onto a stone or tile.
Cook for 10 minutes. Remove the pizzas
from the oven when cooked and golden.
Slice each pizza into eight pieces and serve
immediately, accompanied by the Papaya
and Mango Salsa.

PAPAYA AND MANGO SALSA
Combine the ingredients for the salsa in a
bowl. Vary the amount of chile paste to suit
your taste.

Barbecued Chicken with Sour Cream

~~~

USE OUR BARBECUE SAUCE RECIPE TO BREATHE A LITTLE "FIRE" INTO THIS RECIPE. IT'S MAGNIFICENT WITH A LARGE DOLLOP OF SOUR CREAM HEAPED ON TOP—DEFINITELY A CROWD PLEASER.

13 ounces chicken breast, trimmed of any fat and sinew
a little olive oil
2 cloves garlic, crushed (optional)
2 (8-ounce) dough balls (see page 8)
scant ½ cup Pizza Sauce (see page 10)
¼ cup Barbecue Sauce (see page 11)
1¼ cups grated mozzarella cheese
1 avocado, peeled and cut into pieces
½ pint (4 ounces) cherry tomatoes, halved
5 ounces Swiss cheese, cut into chunks
scant ½ cup sour cream

MAKES 2 MEDIUM PIZZAS

Put the chicken breasts in a bowl. Marinate with a little olive oil and the garlic (if using). Grill or broil the breasts until cooked on both sides. Allow to cool and then slice across the breasts into very thin pieces.

Meanwhile, place two pizza stones or tiles in the oven. Heat the oven to 500°F. Roll out the pizza dough, as described on page 10, so that you have two bases. Cover the bases with the Pizza Sauce and mozzarella cheese, keeping a 1¼-inch border around the edge of the dough clean.

Place the sliced chicken in a random pattern on the bases, leaving spaces for the other ingredients to fall into. Add the avocado, cherry tomatoes, and Swiss cheese.

Using a wide spatula or pizza paddle, gently slide each pizza onto a stone or tile. Cook for 10 minutes. Remove the pizzas from the oven when cooked and golden. Slice each pizza into eight pieces and serve immediately, garnished with the sour cream.

Smoked Turkey with Black Bean & Lime Salsa

~~~

A VISUALLY APPEALING PIZZA, THIS IS OUR VERSION OF
THE "BLT"—BLACK BEAN, LIME, AND TURKEY.

BLACK BEAN AND LIME SALSA

1 cob of fresh corn, husk and silk removed
2 ounces black beans, cooked in salted
   water until tender
1 red onion, finely diced
¼ bunch of coriander (cilantro), freshly
   chopped
juice of 1 lime

PIZZA

2 (8-ounce) dough balls (see page 8)
⅔ cup Pizza Sauce (see page 10)
1¼ cups grated mozzarella cheese
11 ounces smoked turkey, cut into pieces
2 teaspoons sliced jalapeño chile peppers
¾ cup grated provolone cheese (can be
   replaced with mozzarella cheese)
scant ½ cup sour cream (optional)

MAKES 2 MEDIUM PIZZAS

BLACK BEAN AND LIME SALSA

Preheat the oven to 325°F. Wrap the corn cob in foil and roast for 20–30 minutes. Take out of the foil and remove the kernels from the cob with a knife. Combine the corn kernels and the remaining ingredients for the salsa in a bowl. Set aside.

Place two pizza stones or tiles in the oven. Heat the oven to 500°F. Roll out the pizza dough, as described on page 10, so that you have two bases. Cover the bases with the Pizza Sauce and mozzarella cheese, keeping a 1¼-inch border around the edge of the dough clean. Dot the smoked turkey on the bases in a random pattern. Add the jalapeños and small spoonfuls of the Black Bean and Lime Salsa. Sprinkle the provolone cheese over the top.

   Using a wide spatula or pizza paddle, gently slide each pizza onto a stone or tile. Cook for 10 minutes. Remove the pizzas from the oven when cooked and golden. Slice each pizza into eight pieces and serve immediately, garnished with the sour cream (if using).

Tahitian

~~~

THE PAIRING OF CURRY POWDER AND SHREDDED COCONUT IN THIS RECIPE
MAKES AN UNUSUAL BUT TASTY PIZZA.

2 (8-ounce) dough balls (see page 8)
⅔ cup Pizza Sauce (see page 10)
1¼ cups grated mozzarella cheese
5 ounces scallops, seared
7 ounces smoked chicken, shredded
1 small onion, cut into wedges and roasted
  (see page 12)
1 red bell pepper, diced
1 teaspoon curry powder
2 tablespoons shredded (flaked) coconut
3 tablespoons chopped coriander (cilantro)
  leaves
freshly ground black pepper, to taste

MAKES 2 MEDIUM PIZZAS

Place two pizza stones or tiles in the oven. Heat the oven to 500°F. Roll out the pizza dough, as described on page 10, so that you have two bases. Cover the bases with the Pizza Sauce and mozzarella cheese, keeping a 1¼-inch border around the edge of the dough clean.

Place the scallops in a clock-style pattern around the edge of each base. Now dot with the smoked chicken in a random pattern. Place the roast onion and red bell pepper on top. Lightly dust each pizza with the curry powder. Lastly, sprinkle with the coconut and coriander.

Using a wide spatula or pizza paddle, gently slide each pizza onto a stone or tile. Cook for 10 minutes. Remove the pizzas from the oven when cooked and golden. Slice each pizza into eight pieces and season with the ground black pepper. Serve immediately.

Mexican Chicken with Roast Garlic & Chiles

~~~

MOLE, A COMPLEX MEXICAN SAUCE OF CHILE PEPPERS WITH A HINT OF
CHOCOLATE, MAKES THIS A TRULY SENSATIONAL TEX MEX STYLE PIZZA. ADJUST
THE AMOUNT OF JALAPEÑO CHILE PEPPERS TO SUIT YOUR TASTE.

4 teaspoons mole paste (Mexican ground
  spice seasoning, available from Tex Mex
  supply stores or gourmet stores)
scant ½ cup chicken stock
13 ounces chicken breast, trimmed of any
  fat and sinew
2 (8-ounce) dough balls (see page 8)
⅔ cup Pizza Sauce (see page 10)
1¼ cups grated mozzarella cheese
4 teaspoons roast garlic purée (see page 13)
4 teaspoons sliced jalapeño chile peppers,
  or to taste
½ bunch of coriander (cilantro), freshly
  chopped
⅔ cup Guacamole (see page 58)
sour cream, to garnish (optional)

MAKES 2 MEDIUM PIZZAS

Put the mole into a bowl and add enough
of the stock to make a thick sauce. Add the
chicken breasts to this mixture and marinate in the refrigerator for several hours
(overnight is ideal). Roast the chicken in the
oven at 350°F for 10–12 minutes. Allow to
cool and cut across the breast into strips.

Place two pizza stones or tiles in the
oven. Heat the oven to 500°F. Roll out the
pizza dough, as described on page 10, so
that you have two bases.

Cover the bases with the Pizza Sauce and
mozzarella cheese, keeping a 1¼-inch border around the edge of the dough clean. Dot
the chicken on the bases in a random pattern. Place small amounts of the roast garlic
all over the bases. Add the jalapeños and
sprinkle with the coriander.

Using a wide spatula or pizza paddle,
gently slide each pizza onto a stone or tile.
Cook for 10 minutes. Remove the pizzas
from the oven when cooked and golden.
Slice each pizza into eight pieces and garnish with the Guacamole and sour cream
(if using). Serve immediately.

Santa Fe Chicken

~~~

THIS IS A FAIRLY QUICK RECIPE TO THROW TOGETHER. THE FIRE
CONTENT OF JALAPEÑOS VARIES FROM ONE TO ANOTHER, SO TRY
THEM BEFORE BECOMING TOO GENEROUS. YOU WILL ONLY NEED
ABOUT ONE SLICE OF JALAPEÑO PER SLICE OF PIZZA.

2 (8-ounce) dough balls (see page 8)
⅔ cup Pizza Sauce (see page 10)
1¼ cups grated mozzarella cheese
1 cup sun-dried tomatoes (drained of oil),
　cut into chunks
8 ounces chicken, cooked and sliced
　(leftover roast chicken works well
　for this recipe)
1 medium avocado, peeled and cut into
　pieces
1½ ounces Brie cheese, sliced into strips
　about ¼ inch thick
12–16 slices jalapeño chile pepper
½ bunch of coriander (cilantro) leaves,
　chopped

MAKES 2 MEDIUM PIZZAS

Place two pizza stones or tiles in the oven.
Heat the oven to 500°F. Roll out the pizza
dough, as described on page 10, so that
you have two bases. Cover the bases with
the Pizza Sauce and mozzarella cheese,
keeping a 1¼-inch border around the edge
of the dough clean.

Dot the sun-dried tomatoes on the bases.
Next add the chicken in a random pattern,
leaving spaces for the other ingredients
to fall into. Add the avocado, Brie, and
jalapeños. Sprinkle with the coriander.

Using a wide spatula or pizza paddle,
gently slide each pizza onto a stone or tile.
Cook for 10 minutes. Remove the pizzas
from the oven when cooked and golden.
Slice each pizza into eight pieces and serve
immediately.

Smoked Chicken with Corn & Wild Rice

~~~~~~

**TOPPED WITH CREAMED CORN AND WILD RICE INSTEAD OF THE USUAL TOMATO
SAUCE AND MOZZARELLA CHEESE, THIS IS A DELICIOUSLY DIFFERENT PIZZA.**

1 can (14 ounces) creamed corn
1 cup corn
1⅔ cups whipping cream
a little cornstarch
salt and freshly ground black pepper,
   to taste
3–4 tablespoons raw wild rice
2 (8-ounce) dough balls (see page 8)
1 cup sun-dried tomatoes (drained of oil),
   chopped
11 ounces smoked chicken, bones removed
   and chicken cut into slices
½ bunch of coriander (cilantro) leaves,
   chopped (optional)

MAKES 2 MEDIUM PIZZAS

Place the creamed corn, corn, and cream
in a medium saucepan. Heat gently, stirring
constantly, until the mixture comes to the
boil. Add a little cornstarch to thicken the
mixture slightly. Remove from the heat and
season with salt and pepper. Set aside to cool.

Place two pizza stones or tiles in the
oven. Heat the oven to 500°F.

Add the wild rice to a saucepan of water
(use about 4 parts water to 1 part rice).
Bring to the boil and cook for 15–20 minutes. When cooked, drain and add to the
creamed corn mixture.

Roll out the pizza dough, as described on
page 10, so that you have two bases. Cover
the bases with the creamed corn mixture,
keeping a 1¼-inch border around the edge
of the dough clean. Dot the sun-dried tomato
on the bases. Add the chicken in a random
pattern. Sprinkle the coriander over the top
(if using).

Using a wide spatula or pizza paddle,
gently slide each pizza onto a stone or tile.
Cook for 10 minutes. Remove the pizzas
from the oven when cooked and golden.
Slice each pizza into eight pieces and serve
immediately.

Chicken Teriyaki

~~~~~

YOU MAY DECIDE TO MAKE YOUR OWN TERIYAKI SAUCE FOR THIS PIZZA.
IF SO, THERE IS A RECIPE GIVEN FOR THIS UNDER THE ORIENTAL DUCK RECIPE.
IF NOT, SIMPLY USE A SUPERMARKET BRAND.

13 ounces chicken breast, trimmed of any
    fat and sinew
½ cup teriyaki sauce (see page 26)
2 (8-ounce) dough balls (see page 8)
⅔ cup Pizza Sauce (see page 10)
1¼ cups grated mozzarella cheese
1 medium red bell pepper, diced
1 cup bean sprouts
½ bunch of coriander (cilantro), freshly
    chopped

MAKES 2 MEDIUM PIZZAS

Marinate the chicken breasts in the teriyaki sauce for several hours, preferably overnight. Grill the marinated breasts on a barbecue or roast in the oven at 350°F until cooked. Allow to cool and then cut across the breast into slices.

Place two pizza stones or tiles in the oven. Heat the oven to 500°F. Roll out the pizza dough, as described on page 10, so that you have two bases. Cover the bases with the Pizza Sauce and mozzarella cheese, keeping a 1¼-inch border around the edge of the dough clean.

Place the chicken on the bases in a random pattern, leaving spaces for other ingredients to fall into. Add the red bell pepper and bean sprouts. Sprinkle with the coriander.

Using a wide spatula or pizza paddle, gently slide each pizza onto a stone or tile. Cook for 10 minutes. Remove the pizzas from the oven when cooked and golden. Slice each pizza into eight pieces and serve immediately.

Oriental Duck

~~~

THIS PIZZA BECAME SO POPULAR THAT OUR POULTRY SUPPLIER
COULD NOT KEEP UP WITH THE DEMAND OF OUR CUSTOMERS! NOW WE
FEATURE IT FROM TIME TO TIME AS A 'PIZZA OF THE DAY' AND THE USUAL
REACTION FROM CLIENTS AND STAFF IS TO ASK WHY WE DON'T
HAVE THIS PIZZA ON THE MENU ALL THE TIME.

TERIYAKI SAUCE
½ tablespoon sesame oil
¾ ounce fresh ginger, peeled and thinly
    sliced
1 onion, diced
1 teaspoon crushed garlic
2 sprigs fresh rosemary
1¼ cups pineapple juice
¾ cup orange juice
¼ cup honey
¾ cup soy sauce
a little cornstarch

ORIENTAL DUCK
4 duck legs (thigh and drumstick),
    trimmed of fat
1 cup Teriyaki Sauce (see opposite)
approx. 1 cup chicken stock (use the liquid
    variety if using instant stock)

PIZZA
1 ounce dried shiitake or Chinese
    mushrooms
1 tablespoon honey
2 (8-ounce) dough balls (see page 8)
⅔ cup Pizza Sauce (see page 10)
1¼ cups grated mozzarella cheese
⅔ cup bean sprouts
2 small scallions, thinly sliced on the angle,
    Chinese style
finely grated peel of 1 orange
sesame seeds, toasted (optional)

MAKES 2 MEDIUM PIZZAS

TERIYAKI SAUCE
Heat the sesame oil gently over a moderate
heat in a medium saucepan. Add the ginger,
onion, garlic, and rosemary. Sauté until the
onion is transparent, then add the pineapple
and orange juices, honey, and soy sauce.
Bring to a boil and thicken slightly with
a little cornstarch. Set aside to cool.

ORIENTAL DUCK

Preheat the oven to 300°F.

You will need to score the flesh of the duck before cooking so the marinade will penetrate through to the bone. Using a sharp knife, make several cuts across the leg, 1¼–1½ inches long. Place the duck in a shallow pan and add ⅔ cup Teriyaki Sauce and chicken stock. (The liquid should come halfway up the duck.)

Place the duck in the oven and cook for 1–1½ hours. When cooked, the flesh should fall off the bone easily. Remove the duck from the cooking liquid and allow to cool. Remove and discard any skin, and shred the meat from the bones. You will need 7 ounces of shredded meat for the pizza.

Reconstitute the mushrooms by placing them in a saucepan and covering with water. Add the honey and cover the pan. Simmer gently for 30–40 minutes, until the mushrooms are soft. Remove from the heat and drain. When cool, slice into thin strips.

Place two pizza stones or tiles in the oven. Heat the oven to 500°F. Roll out the pizza dough, as described on page 10, so that you have two bases. Cover the bases with the Pizza Sauce and mozzarella cheese, keeping a 1¼-inch border around the edge of the dough clean.

Place the duck on the bases in a random pattern, leaving spaces for other ingredients to fall into. Add the bean sprouts, scallions, and mushrooms. Drizzle some of the remaining Teriyaki Sauce over the top, remembering to keep the edges of the pizzas clean. Be conservative when applying this sauce as it is fairly strong. Finally, sprinkle the orange peel over the top.

Using a wide spatula or pizza paddle, gently slide each pizza onto a stone or tile. Cook for 10 minutes. Remove the pizzas from the oven when cooked and golden. Sprinkle some sesame seeds over the pizzas as a garnish (if using). Slice each pizza into eight pieces and serve immediately.

Mediterranean Chicken

~~~

WITH TASTES FROM THE SUN-DRENCHED ISLANDS OF GREECE, THIS PIZZA
USES TOMATOES, OLIVES, GARLIC, AND BOCCONCINI CHEESE TO PRODUCE
A FLAVORFUL MARRIAGE OF INGREDIENTS.

8 ounces chicken breast, trimmed of any
   fat and sinew
2 tablespoons olive oil
2 cloves garlic, crushed
salt and freshly ground black pepper,
   to taste
grated peel of 1 lemon
1½ teaspoons chopped lemon thyme leaves
2 (8-ounce) dough balls (see page 8)
⅔ cup Pizza Sauce (see page 10)
1¼ cups grated mozzarella cheese
1 cup sun-dried tomatoes (drained of oil),
   roughly chopped
½ large onion, cut into wedges and roasted
   (see page 12)
¼ cup kalamata olives, pitted and
   quartered
2½ ounces bocconcini cheese, cut into
   ½-inch slices
½ bunch of basil, finely sliced

MAKES 2 MEDIUM PIZZAS

Preheat the oven to 350°F. Place the chicken in a bowl. Combine the olive oil and garlic, and rub over the chicken. Place in a roasting pan and cook in the oven for 12–15 minutes. Remove the chicken from the oven, but do not turn the oven off. When the chicken is cool, cut it into pieces, slicing across the breast. Place in a bowl and season with salt and pepper. Add the lemon peel and lemon thyme. Mix together.

Place two pizza stones or tiles in the oven. Heat the oven to 500°F. Roll out the pizza dough, as described on page 10, so that you have two bases. Cover the bases with the Pizza Sauce and mozzarella cheese, keeping a 1¼-inch border around the edge of the dough clean. Dot with the sun-dried tomatoes first. Add the chicken pieces in a random pattern, leaving spaces for other ingredients to fall into. Add the onion, olives, and bocconcini cheese. Top with the basil.

Using a wide spatula or pizza paddle, gently slide each pizza onto a stone or tile. Cook for 10 minutes. Remove the pizzas from the oven when cooked and golden. Slice each pizza into eight pieces and serve immediately.

Wild Mushroom, Chicken, Pine Nuts, & Thyme

~~~

AN EARTHY, RUSTIC PIZZA COMBINING BASIC FLAVORS THAT COMPLEMENT
EACH OTHER WELL. THE THYME CAN BE REPLACED WITH LEMON THYME TO
ADD ANOTHER DIMENSION IN TASTE AND FRAGRANCE.

2 (8-ounce) dough balls (see page 8)

⅔ cup Pizza Sauce (see page 10)

1¼ cups grated mozzarella cheese

a little olive oil

1½ pounds field or oyster or shimeji mushrooms, cut into ¼-inch slices

¼ bunch of thyme, stems discarded and
 leaves chopped

salt and freshly ground black pepper,
 to taste

13 ounces chicken breast, trimmed of any
 fat and sinew, roasted and sliced

6 scallions, sliced on the angle, Chinese
 style

¼ cup pine nuts, toasted

MAKES 2 MEDIUM PIZZAS

Place two pizza stones or tiles in the oven. Heat the oven to 500°F. Roll out the pizza dough, as described on page 10, so that you have two bases. Cover the bases with the Pizza Sauce and mozzarella cheese, keeping a 1¼-inch border around the edge of the dough clean.

Heat the olive oil in a pan until quite hot. Add the mushrooms and sauté for 2–3 minutes. Add the thyme and season with salt and pepper. Remove the mushrooms from the pan and drain on paper towels.

Place the chicken on the bases in a random pattern, leaving spaces for other ingredients to fall into. Add the mushrooms, scallions, and pine nuts.

Using a wide spatula or pizza paddle, gently slide each pizza onto a stone or tile. Cook for 10 minutes. Remove the pizzas from the oven when cooked and golden. Slice each pizza into eight pieces and serve immediately.

Thai Chicken

〜

A RELATIVELY SIMPLE RECIPE THAT HAS GRADUALLY EVOLVED WITH
EACH NEW MENU AT THE RESTAURANT TO BECOME A BALANCE OF HOT AND
TASTY. IF YOU PREFER A MILDER FLAVOR, SIMPLY REDUCE THE
AMOUNT OF RED CURRY PASTE USED IN THE SAUCE.

THAI SAUCE
1 teaspoon vegetable oil
2 teaspoons red curry paste
2 tablespoons brown sugar
1 can (13 ounces) coconut milk
1 teaspoon dried lemon grass
juice and grated peel of 1 lime
4 teaspoons cornstarch
a little water
¾ cup crunchy peanut butter
4 teaspoons fish sauce *(nam pla)*

PIZZA
13 ounces chicken breast, trimmed of any
   fat and sinew
a little oil
2 (8-ounce) dough balls (see page 8)
1¼ cups grated mozzarella cheese
1 medium carrot, cut into fine julienne
1 cup bean sprouts
5 scallions, sliced on the angle, Chinese
   style
½ bunch of coriander (cilantro) leaves,
   picked and chopped

MAKES 2 MEDIUM PIZZAS

THAI SAUCE
Heat the vegetable oil in a medium
saucepan over a medium heat. Add the
curry paste and stir through. Stir in the
sugar and mix well. Add the coconut milk,
lemon grass, and lime juice and peel. Bring
to the boil.

Make a paste of the cornstarch with a
little water. Stir into the sauce to thicken
slightly. Strain this mixture and then add the
peanut butter and the fish sauce. Set aside
to cool.

Place the chicken breasts in a bowl or shallow dish. Add enough of the Thai Sauce to
marinate the chicken. Cover and leave in the
refrigerator overnight. (The leftover sauce
can be stored in an airtight container in the
refrigerator until needed for the base sauce.)

Preheat the oven to 325°F. Place the
chicken breasts on a lightly oiled oven tray
or baking sheet. Roast for 12–15 minutes.
Remove the chicken from the oven and allow
the chicken to cool completely. Slice into
strips across the breast. Use some of the Thai
Sauce to moisten the chicken slightly.

Place two pizza stones or tiles in the oven. Heat the oven to 500°F. Roll out the pizza dough, as described on page 10, so that you have two bases. Cover the bases with the Thai Sauce and mozzarella cheese, keeping a 1¼-inch border around the edge of the dough clean.

Place the chicken on the bases in a random pattern, leaving spaces for other ingredients to fall into. Add the carrot, bean sprouts, and scallions. Sprinkle the coriander over the top.

Using a wide spatula or pizza paddle, gently slide each pizza onto a stone or tile. Cook for 10 minutes. Remove the pizzas from the oven when cooked and golden. Slice each pizza into eight pieces and serve immediately.

Smoked Chicken, Eggplant, Roma Tomatoes, Provolone, & Basil

〜

THIS PIZZA HAS ITS OWN TOMATO SAUCE BASE—ONE WITHOUT THE
SPICE CONTENT OF THE REGULAR PIZZA SAUCE—TO ALLOW THE SUBTLE
FLAVORS OF THE TOPPINGS TO BE FULLY APPRECIATED. THE
SMOKED CHICKEN CAN BE REPLACED WITH LEFTOVER ROAST
CHICKEN OR EVEN SMOKED HAM IF YOU PREFER.

TOMATO SAUCE

1 can (14 ounces) good-quality crushed
  tomatoes
2 teaspoons olive oil
1 yellow onion, finely diced
1 teaspoon crushed garlic
4 basil leaves, finely sliced

PIZZA

2 (8-ounce) dough balls (see page 8)
⅔ cup Tomato Sauce (see above)
1¼ cups grated mozzarella cheese
13 ounces smoked chicken or leftover roast
  chicken, shredded or sliced into pieces
1 small eggplant, cut into slices ½ inch
  thick and roasted (see page 102)
2 small Roma (plum) tomatoes, sliced into
  ¼-inch rings

4 ounces provolone cheese, cut into chunks
8 basil leaves, finely sliced
freshly ground black pepper, to taste

MAKES 2 MEDIUM PIZZAS

TOMATO SAUCE

Put the crushed tomatoes into a saucepan
over a medium heat. Reduce the tomatoes
in volume by half. Heat the olive oil in a
separate pan over a medium heat. Add the
onion and garlic. Sauté until transparent.
Add the basil and sauté for another minute
before adding the reduced tomatoes. Mix
thoroughly. Remove from the heat and allow
to cool.

Place two pizza stones or tiles in the oven. Heat the oven to 500°F. Roll out the pizza dough, as described on page 10, so that you have two bases. Cover the bases with the Tomato Sauce and mozzarella cheese, keeping a 1¼-inch border around the edge of the dough clean.

Place the smoked chicken on the bases in a random pattern, leaving spaces for other ingredients to fall into. Cut the eggplant slices into quarters and place on the bases in a random pattern. Add the tomato. Scatter the provolone cheese over the top.

Using a wide spatula or pizza paddle, gently slide each pizza onto a stone or tile. Cook for 10 minutes. Remove the pizza from the oven when cooked and golden. Slice each pizza into eight pieces and sprinkle the basil over the top. Serve immediately, garnished with the black pepper.

Barbecued Chicken with Flat-Leaf Parsley, Barbecued Corn, & Mint

~~~

THE CHICKEN IS BEST COOKED ON THE GRILL BARS OF A BARBECUE TO GIVE IT THAT DISTINCTIVE SMOKY, CHARRED FLAVOR. THE CORN CAN BE COOKED AT THE SAME TIME.

4 teaspoons olive oil

1 teaspoon crushed garlic

2 teaspoons chopped fresh flat-leaf (Italian) parsley

2 large chicken breasts, trimmed of any fat and sinew

salt and freshly ground black pepper, to taste

2 medium corn cobs, husks and silks removed

a little butter

2 (8-ounce) dough balls (see page 8)

⅔ cup Pizza Sauce (see page 10)

1¼ cups grated mozzarella cheese

8 mint leaves, freshly chopped

sour cream, to garnish (optional)

a little Tabasco sauce (optional)

MAKES 2 MEDIUM PIZZAS

Put the olive oil in a small bowl. Add the garlic and parsley. Pound the chicken breasts so that they are the same thickness all over. Season with salt and pepper. Marinate the breasts in the olive oil mixture.

Bring a saucepan of salted water to the boil. Add the corn cobs. Simmer for 10–15 minutes, depending on size. Remove from the pan and drain.

Wrap each corn cob in foil with a little butter, salt, and pepper. Place the foiled corn on the grill bars of your barbecue. Roast over a medium heat for 10 minutes, turning every 3 minutes or so. Remove the corn from the barbecue and open the foil.

When the corn is cool enough to handle, take a small, sharp knife and cut the kernels off the cobs. It will be easier if you slice the cob in half and then straighten the end. This way you will be able to stand the cob on its end and slice straight down. Set the corn kernels aside.

Meanwhile, place the chicken breasts on the grill. Sear for about 2 minutes, before turning the breasts 90 degrees and cooking for another 2 minutes. This will make a criss-cross pattern on the chicken. Turn the breasts over and repeat the process. Remove from the barbecue and allow to cool. Cut into slices about ¼-inch thick.

Place two pizza stones or tiles in the oven. Heat the oven to 500°F. Roll out the pizza dough, as described on page 10, so that you have two bases. Cover the bases with the Pizza Sauce and mozzarella cheese, keeping a 1¼-inch border around the edge of the dough clean.

Place the chicken on the bases in a random pattern. Sprinkle generously with the corn kernels. (Some extra mozzarella cheese over the top will help hold the topping in place.)

Using a wide spatula or pizza paddle, gently slide each pizza onto a stone or tile. Cook for 10 minutes. Remove from the oven when cooked and golden. Slice each pizza into eight pieces. Sprinkle the mint over the top and season with black pepper. Garnish with a dollop of sour cream and a few splashes of Tabasco (if using). Serve immediately.

Grilled Chicken, Goat Cheese, Roast Peppers, Pine Nuts, & Raisins

~~~

THE ACIDITY OF THE GOAT CHEESE ON THIS PIZZA PROVIDES A WONDERFUL
COMPLEMENT TO THE SWEETNESS OF THE ROAST PEPPERS. IT BLENDS WITH
THE PINE NUTS AND RAISINS TO MAKE A LUSCIOUS, CREAMY PIZZA.
BE SURE TO TOP WITH A FEW GRINDS OF FRESH BLACK PEPPER.

2 (8-ounce) dough balls (see page 8)
⅔ cup Pizza Sauce (see page 10)
1¼ cups grated mozzarella cheese
13 ounces chicken breast, trimmed of any
   fat and sinew, cooked and sliced
3 ounces goat cheese
1 red bell pepper, roasted and cut into
   chunks (see page 12)
¼ cup pine nuts
3 tablespoons raisins, soaked in warm
   water to soften

MAKES 2 MEDIUM PIZZAS

Place two pizza stones or tiles in the oven. Heat the oven to 500°F. Roll out the pizza dough, as described on page 10, so that you have two bases. Cover the bases with the Pizza Sauce and mozzarella cheese, keeping a 1¼-inch border around the edge of the dough clean.

Dot the chicken on the bases in a random pattern. Add the goat cheese, red bell pepper, pine nuts, and raisins.

Using a wide spatula or pizza paddle, gently slide each pizza onto a stone or tile. Cook for 10 minutes. Remove the pizzas from the oven when cooked and golden. Slice each pizza into eight pieces and serve immediately.

Pizza con CARNE

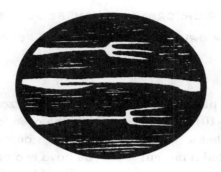

THE TOPPINGS IN THIS CHAPTER ENCOMPASS A WIDE
RANGE OF MEATS—FROM BEEF, LAMB, AND PORK
TO SALAMI, SAUSAGE, AND PROSCIUTTO. ALL RECIPES
ASSUME THAT ANY FAT HAS BEEN REMOVED FROM FRESH
MEAT, INCLUDING SINEW AND GRISTLE.

WHEN COOKING PIECES OF MEAT FOR PIZZA TOPPINGS,
WHETHER THEY BE STRIPS OR MEDALLIONS, BE SURE TO
KEEP THE MEAT UNDERCOOKED OR "PINK" IN THE MIDDLE.
DON'T WORRY, AS IT WILL BE COOKED FURTHER WHEN
THE PIZZA IS BAKED.

WHERE POSSIBLE, USE THE RECOMMENDED CUTS OF MEAT,
AS SUBSTITUTIONS MAY NOT NECESSARILY GIVE THE SAME
RESULT. IF IN DOUBT, ASK YOUR BUTCHER.

Ham, Brie, & Spinach

~~~

A TYPICAL FLORENTINE BREAKFAST OR LUNCHEON SPECIAL. ALTHOUGH
BRIE CHEESE REPLACES THE TRADITIONAL EGG, THIS PIZZA STILL RETAINS
THAT SIGNATURE RICH, CREAMY FINISH. BE SURE TO FINISH WITH A
FEW GRINDS OF FRESH BLACK PEPPER.

2 (8-ounce) dough balls (see page 8)
⅔ cup Pizza Sauce (see page 10)
1¼ cups grated mozzarella cheese
7 ounces sliced double-smoked ham, cut
  into quarters
1 small red onion, cut into quarters and
  roasted (see page 12)
3 ounces Brie cheese, cut into slices ¼-inch
  thick
16 baby spinach leaves, stems removed
a little olive oil
½ teaspoon cumin seeds (optional)

MAKES 2 MEDIUM PIZZAS

Place two pizza stones or tiles in the oven. Heat the oven to 500°F. Roll out the pizza dough, as described on page 10, so that you have two bases. Cover the bases with the Pizza Sauce and mozzarella cheese, keeping 1¼-inch border from the edge of the dough clean.

Place the ham on the bases in a random pattern, leaving spaces for other ingredients to fall into. Add the onion. Break the slices of Brie into 1¼-inch lengths and place on the pizza. Put the spinach leaves in a bowl and drizzle with a little olive oil. Toss the leaves thoroughly to coat them and then place on the pizza. Sprinkle the cumin seeds over the top (if using).

Using a wide spatula or pizza paddle, gently slide each pizza onto a stone or tile. Cook for 10 minutes. Remove the pizzas from the oven when cooked and golden. Slice each pizza into eight pieces and serve immediately.

Black Bean Beef

~~~

INSPIRED BY CHINESE CUISINE, THIS PIZZA GETS ITS PRINCIPAL
FLAVOR FROM CARAMELIZING THE BLACK BEAN SAUCE AROUND THE BEEF.
IT CARRIES A DISTINCTIVE FLAVOR WHICH I AM SURE YOU'VE ENCOUNTERED
IN THE PAST, EVEN IF NOT NECESSARILY ON A PIZZA!

11 ounces topside or rump beef, cut into
strips about 1¼ inches × ½ inch

4 teaspoons black bean sauce (available
from good supermarkets or Asian
food stores)

a little vegetable oil

1 teaspoon sesame oil

2 (8-ounce) dough balls (see page 8)

⅔ cup Pizza Sauce (see page 10)

1¼ cups grated mozzarella cheese

3 scallions, sliced on the angle, Chinese
style

½ cup cashew nuts, roughly chopped

1½ cups bean sprouts

¼ bunch of coriander (cilantro), freshly
chopped

1 tablespoon sesame seeds, toasted

MAKES 2 MEDIUM PIZZAS

Marinate the beef in the black bean sauce
for at least 2 hours. Pour a little vegetable
oil into a medium frying pan or wok. Add
the sesame oil and heat until the oil begins
to shimmer. Add the beef strips, taking care
to avoid splashing yourself with the oil. Stir-
fry for about 3 minutes, sealing the meat on
all sides. Remove from the pan and allow
to cool.

Place two pizza stones or tiles in the
oven. Heat the oven to 500°F. Roll out the
pizza dough, as described on page 10, so
that you have two bases. Cover the bases
with the Pizza Sauce and mozzarella cheese,
keeping a 1¼-inch border around the edge
of the dough clean.

Place the beef on the bases in a random
pattern, leaving spaces for the other ingredients to fall into. Add the scallions, cashews,
and bean sprouts. Sprinkle the coriander
over the top.

Using a wide spatula or pizza paddle,
gently slide each pizza onto a stone or tile.
Cook for 10 minutes. Remove the pizzas from
the oven when cooked and golden. Slice
each pizza into eight pieces and serve immediately, garnished with the sesame seeds.

Marinated Lamb Fillets with Pesto

~~~

THIS PIZZA IS ESPECIALLY GOOD FOR THOSE OF YOU WHO ENJOY
GARLIC-MARINATED LAMB ON A KEBAB-STYLE PIZZA.

3 teaspoons olive oil
1 teaspoon crushed garlic
10 ounces lamb tenderloin, trimmed of any
    fat and sinew
2 (8-ounce) dough balls (see page 8)
⅔ cup Pizza Sauce (see page 10)
1¼ cups grated mozzarella cheese
⅓ cup Pesto Sauce (see page 11)
1 red bell pepper, roasted, peeled, and
    seeded, then cut into large chunks
freshly chopped basil
a little tabbouleh, or cucumber and
    yogurt, to garnish (optional)

MAKES 2 MEDIUM PIZZAS

Combine the olive oil and garlic. Marinate the lamb in this mixture for several hours in the refrigerator.

Preheat the oven to 400°F. Heat a frying pan or skillet until quite hot. Add the lamb and quickly sear on all sides to seal in the juices (just long enough to color the meat). Remove from the pan immediately.

Roast the lamb in the oven for about 5 minutes. (The cut of meat you use will dictate the length of the cooking time. As a general guide, the thicker the piece, the longer you will have to cook it. With lamb, the meat should still be pink; it is going back into the oven, so leave it slightly undercooked. If the lamb is cooked until rare now, it will be medium to rare once cooked on the pizza.) Alternatively, for extra flavor, cook the lamb on a barbecue. Allow to cool and then cut into slices about ¼-inch thick. Set aside.

Place two pizza stones or tiles in the oven and increase the oven temperature to 500°F.

Roll out the pizza dough, as described on page 10, so that you have two bases.

Cover the bases with the Pizza Sauce and mozzarella cheese, keeping a 1¼-inch border around the edge of the dough clean.

Place the lamb on the bases in a random pattern, leaving spaces for other ingredients to fall into. Using a teaspoon, dot small dollops of Pesto Sauce around each pizza. Add the roast red bell pepper and sprinkle some chopped basil over the top.

Using a wide spatula or pizza paddle, gently slide each pizza onto a stone or tile. Cook for 10 minutes. Remove the pizzas from the oven when cooked and golden. Slice each pizza into eight pieces. Serve immediately, garnished with the tabbouleh or cucumber and yogurt (if using).

Pepperoni

~~~

DURING THE EVOLUTION OF THIS PIZZA, WE EXPERIMENTED WITH SEVERAL DIFFERENT TYPES OF PEPPERONI. WE NOW USE A MIXTURE OF HOT AND MILD PEPPERONI TO ACHIEVE A TASTY COMBINATION. SAMPLE A FEW DIFFERENT TYPES TO FIND THE COMBINATION YOU PREFER.

2 (8-ounce) dough balls (see page 8)
⅔ cup Pizza Sauce (see page 10)
1¼ cups grated mozzarella cheese
3 ounces pepperoni, thinly sliced
5 ounces button mushrooms, thinly sliced
½ cup kalamata olives, pitted and cut into
    quarters
extra mozzarella cheese, grated

MAKES 2 MEDIUM PIZZAS

Place two pizza stones or tiles in the oven. Heat the oven to 500°F. Roll out the pizza dough, as described on page 10, so that you have two bases. Cover the bases with the Pizza Sauce and mozzarella cheese, keeping a 1¼-inch border around the edge of the dough clean.

Place the pepperoni on the bases in a random pattern, leaving spaces for other ingredients to fall into. Add the mushrooms and olives. Sprinkle some extra mozzarella cheese over the top.

Using a wide spatula or pizza paddle, gently slide each pizza onto a stone or tile. Cook for 10 minutes. Remove the pizzas from the oven when cooked and golden. Slice each pizza into eight pieces and serve immediately.

Spinach, Pancetta, & Cashews with Feta

~~~

THE INTENSE FLAVORS OF THE PANCETTA AND SUN-DRIED TOMATOES ARE
CUT BY THE CREAMY FETA CHEESE, MAKING A FULL-BODIED PIZZA
TOPPED WITH CRISP, ROASTED CASHEWS.

2 (8-ounce) dough balls (see page 8)
⅔ cup Pizza Sauce (see page 10)
1¼ cups grated mozzarella cheese
1 ounce pancetta or prosciutto slices, cut
   into pieces about 1¼ inches × ½ inch.
⅔ cup sun-dried tomatoes (drained of oil),
   cut into chunks
¼ cup unsalted roasted cashew nuts,
   roughly chopped
3 ounces feta cheese
16 baby spinach leaves, stems removed
   and leaves rubbed with a little olive oil

MAKES 2 MEDIUM PIZZAS

Place two pizza stones or tiles in the oven. Heat the oven to 500°F. Roll out the pizza dough, as described on page 10, so that you have two bases. Cover the bases with the Pizza Sauce and mozzarella cheese, keeping a 1¼-inch border around the edge of the dough clean.

Place the pancetta in a clock-style pattern around the edge of each base, with 2 pieces in the middle. Add the sun-dried tomatoes, cashews, and feta. Place the spinach leaves over the top.

Using a wide spatula or pizza paddle, gently slide each pizza onto a stone or tile. Cook for 10 minutes. Remove the pizzas from the oven when cooked and golden. Slice each pizza into eight pieces and serve immediately.

Roast Beef, Sautéed Potato, & Caramelized Onion with Béarnaise Sauce

~~~

A PERSONAL FAVORITE. A PIZZA MAY NOT BE THE PLACE YOU EXPECT TO FIND ROAST FILLET OF BEEF, BUT IT IS A MOUTHWATERING TREAT. DON'T FORGET THE ALMOST OBLIGATORY GRINDS OF FRESH BLACK PEPPER.

BÉARNAISE SAUCE
a little butter
1 yellow onion, finely diced
1 large sprig French tarragon, finely chopped
⅓ cup dry white wine
⅓ cup white wine vinegar
6 egg yolks
¼ pound plus 6 tablespoons (1¾ sticks) butter, melted
salt, to taste
juice of ½ lemon
extra French tarragon, freshly chopped

PIZZA
a little olive oil
13 ounces beef tenderloin or sirloin
2 (8-ounce) dough balls (see page 8)
⅔ cup Pizza Sauce (see page 10)
1¼ cups grated mozzarella cheese

4 medium potatoes, peeled and boiled
1 red onion, cut into wedges and roasted (see page 12)
½ bunch of chives, chopped
freshly ground black pepper, to taste

MAKES 2 MEDIUM PIZZAS

BÉARNAISE SAUCE
Melt a little butter in a small saucepan and add the onion and French tarragon. Sauté until the onion is transparent and then add the white wine and vinegar. Bring to the boil over a medium heat and simmer gently until reduced in volume to about 3 tablespoons. Strain the liquid through a fine sieve.

Put the egg yolks in a medium stainless steel bowl and add the reduced liquid. Place a saucepan of warm water on the stove (the pan must be large enough for the stainless steel bowl to sit in, without the water touching the bottom of the bowl). Bring the water to a gentle simmer and place the bowl on top of the pan (this is known as a bain-marie or water bath). Reduce the heat under the water to very low.

Whisk the egg mixture continuously until it has doubled in volume. Heat the melted butter and drizzle over the egg mixture, whisking constantly, until about four fifths of the butter is incorporated. The sauce should now be nice and thick.

Season with a little salt and add the lemon juice and extra tarragon. Whisk thoroughly to combine and set aside until ready to use. (Only add the remaining melted butter if the sauce if still too thin after adding the lemon juice.)

Preheat the oven to 400°F. Heat a little olive oil in a frying pan or skillet until very hot. Add the beef and quickly sear on all sides to seal in the juices. Remove from the pan and roast in the oven for 5 minutes. Allow the

beef to cool completely before slicing into pieces about ¼ inch thick. Set aside.

Place two pizza stones or tiles in the oven. Heat the oven to 500°F. Roll out the pizza dough, as described on page 10, so that you have two bases. Cover the bases with the Pizza Sauce and mozzarella cheese, keeping a 1¼-inch border around the edge of the dough clean.

Cut the potatoes into quarters. Sauté in a frying pan or skillet with a little olive oil until they are crisp and crunchy in texture. Place the potatoes on the bases in a random pattern, and then add the roast onion (the beef will go on the pizza halfway through cooking).

Using a wide spatula or pizza paddle, gently slide each pizza onto a stone or tile. Cook for 5 minutes. Now place the pieces of beef on the pizzas, and cook for a further 4 minutes. Remove the pizzas from the oven when cooked and golden. Slice each pizza into eight pieces. Spoon the Béarnaise Sauce generously over the top. Serve immediately garnished with the chives and seasoned with the black pepper.

Hawaiian

〜〜〜

A SIMPLE, TRIED, AND TRUE COMBINATION THAT REMAINS POPULAR WITH ALL AGE GROUPS.

2 (8-ounce) dough balls (see page 8)
⅔ cup Pizza Sauce (see page 10)
1¾ cups grated mozzarella cheese
1 medium pineapple, peeled and cut into
    ½-inch cubes
7 ounces sliced double-smoked ham, cut
    into strips ¼ inch wide and 1¼ inches long

MAKES 2 MEDIUM PIZZAS

Place two pizza stones or tiles in the oven. Heat the oven to 500°F. Roll out the pizza dough, as described on page 10, so that you have two bases. Cover the bases with the Pizza Sauce and 1¼ cups of the mozzarella cheese, keeping a 1¼-inch border around the edge of the dough clean.

Place the pineapple on the bases in a random pattern, leaving gaps for the ham to fall into. Add the ham and sprinkle the remaining mozzarella cheese over the top.

Using a wide spatula or pizza paddle, gently slide each pizza onto a stone or tile. Cook for 10 minutes. Remove the pizzas from the oven when cooked and golden. Slice each pizza into eight pieces and serve immediately.

Prosciutto with Eggplant & Sun-dried Tomatoes

~~~~

THIS PIZZA IS AN ADVENTUROUS BUT SATISFYING COMBINATION OF SHARP,
ROBUST TASTES AND SUBTLE FLAVORS.

1 medium eggplant
a little olive oil
salt and freshly ground black pepper,
  to taste
2 (8-ounce) dough balls (see page 8)
⅔ cup Pizza Sauce (see page 10)
1¼ cups grated mozzarella cheese
⅔ cup sun-dried tomatoes (drained of oil),
  chopped
1 ounce sliced prosciutto, rind removed
  and cut into strips about 1¼ inches wide
4 ounces goat cheese, cut into chunks
1 tablespoon kalamata olives, pitted and
  cut into quarters
½ bunch of basil, freshly chopped

MAKES 2 MEDIUM PIZZAS

Preheat the oven to 325°. Slice the eggplant into pieces about ½ inch thick. Place the slices on a lightly oiled baking tray or sheet. Season with salt and pepper. Cover with wax paper. Roast in the oven for 10–15 minutes or until soft. Cut any large pieces into halves or quarters.

Place two pizza stones or tiles in the oven. Heat the oven to 500°F. Roll out the pizza dough, as described on page 10, so that you have two bases. Cover the bases with the Pizza Sauce and mozzarella cheese, keeping a 1¼-inch border around the edge of the dough clean.

Place the sun-dried tomatoes on the bases first so that they do not burn. Add the eggplant in a random pattern, leaving spaces for other ingredients to fall into. Place the prosciutto on the pizzas. Add the goat cheese and olives. Sprinkle the basil over the top.

Using a wide spatula or pizza paddle, gently slide each pizza onto a stone or tile. Cook for 10 minutes. Remove from the oven when cooked and golden. Slice each pizza into eight. Serve immediately.

Spicy Lamb Sausage with Coriander

~~~

THIS PIZZA HAS A MIDDLE EASTERN FLAVOR. USE A TASTY LAMB SAUSAGE
FOR THE TOPPING, PERHAPS ONE CONTAINING GARLIC OR PAPRIKA,
TO COMPLEMENT THE OTHER INGREDIENTS.

2 (8-ounce) dough balls (see page 8)

⅔ cup Pizza Sauce (see page 10)

1¼ cups grated mozzarella cheese

7 ounces spicy lamb sausage, sliced and
    seared in a frying pan or skillet

1 medium eggplant, cut into slices ¼ inch
    thick and roasted (see page 103), then
    quartered

1 large red bell pepper, roasted (see page
    12) and cut into chunks

1 red onion, sliced into rings

¼ bunch of coriander (cilantro), freshly
    chopped

MAKES 2 MEDIUM PIZZAS

Place two pizza stones or tiles in the oven.
Heat the oven to 500°F. Roll out the pizza
dough, as described on page 10, so that
you have two bases. Cover the bases with
the Pizza Sauce and mozzarella cheese,
keeping a 1¼-inch border around the edge
of the dough clean.

Place the sausage slices on the bases in a
random pattern. Add the eggplant and red
bell pepper. Lay the onion rings over the top
and sprinkle with the coriander.

Using a wide spatula or pizza paddle,
gently slide each pizza onto a stone or tile.
Cook for 10 minutes. Remove the pizzas
from the oven when cooked and golden.
Slice each pizza into eight pieces and serve
immediately.

Pepperoni & Salami with Roast Pepper & Onion

~~~

EVEN THE MOST ADVENTURESOME PIZZA CONNOISSEURS ENJOY THE
OCCASIONAL CLASSIC TOPPING COMBINATION SUCH AS THIS ONE. CHOOSE
GOOD-QUALITY SPICY PEPPERONI AND SALAMI FOR THIS PIZZA.

2 (8-ounce) dough balls (see page 8)
⅔ cup Pizza Sauce (see page 10)
1¼ cups grated mozzarella cheese
2 ounces pepperoni, sliced
2 ounces salami, sliced
1 red bell pepper, roasted and cut into
  chunks (see page 12)
1 red onion, sliced into thin rings

MAKES 2 MEDIUM PIZZAS

Place two pizza stones or tiles in the oven. Heat the oven to 500°F. Roll out the pizza dough, as described on page 10, so that you have two bases. Cover the bases with the Pizza Sauce and mozzarella cheese, keeping a 1¼-inch border around the edge of the dough clean.

Place the pepperoni and salami on the bases in a random pattern, leaving spaces for other ingredients to fall into. Add the roast red bell pepper and onion rings.

Using a wide spatula or pizza paddle, gently slide each pizza onto a stone or tile. Cook for 10 minutes. Remove the pizzas from the oven when cooked and golden. Slice each pizza into eight pieces and serve immediately.

Spicy Mexican Beef with Jalapeños

THIS IS A TRADITIONAL-STYLE MEXICAN RECIPE WHERE THE BEEF IS SIMMERED OVER A LOW HEAT FOR 2–3 HOURS. THE "FIRE" RATING OF THIS DISH IS HOT, BUT CAN BE TAMED DOWN TO SUIT YOUR TASTE IF YOU CAN'T STAND THE HEAT!

SPICY MEXICAN BEEF

13 ounces top round steak, cut into strips about 1¼ inches long and ½ inch wide
salt, to taste
a little olive oil
1 yellow onion, diced
1 green bell pepper, diced
½ teaspoon chile paste
½ teaspoon crushed garlic
pinch each of ground cinnamon, cayenne (red) pepper, and ground cloves
1 can (14 ounces) crushed tomatoes
1 teaspoon malt or balsamic vinegar
4 teaspoons tomato paste
2 bay leaves
2 teaspoons sliced jalapeño chile peppers, or to taste

PIZZA

2 (8-ounce) dough balls (see page 8)
3 cups Spicy Mexican Beef (see above)
1¾ cups grated mozzarella cheese

handful of corn chips, broken up roughly
3 scallions, sliced on the angle, Chinese style
1 teaspoon dried chile flakes
sour cream, to garnish

MAKES 2 MEDIUM PIZZAS

SPICY MEXICAN BEEF

Put the sliced beef in a medium saucepan and add enough water to barely cover the meat. Season with salt. Bring to the boil and simmer gently over a medium heat until all the water has evaporated and the meat begins to cook in its own juices. This is a slow process, but it is most important to reduce the liquid gradually and gently.

Heat a little olive oil in a separate saucepan. Add the onion, bell pepper, chile paste, garlic, cinnamon, cayenne, and cloves. Sauté until the onion is transparent.

Add the crushed tomatoes, vinegar, tomato paste, and bay leaves.

Add the meat and bring the mixture to the boil over a gentle heat. Stir thoroughly and then add the jalapeño peppers. Remove from the heat and allow to cool before using. The meat should now have a shredded look and be broken down throughout the sauce.

Place two pizza stones or tiles in the oven. Heat the oven to 500°F. Roll out the pizza dough, as described on page 10, so that you have two bases.

Spoon the Spicy Mexican Beef directly onto the bases, keeping a 1¼-inch border around the edge of the dough clean. Top with 1¼ cups of the mozzarella cheese. Sprinkle the corn chips and scallions over the pizzas. Top with the remaining mozzarella. Now dust the dried chile flakes over the top.

Using a wide spatula or pizza paddle, gently slide each pizza onto a stone or tile. Cook for 10 minutes. Remove the pizzas from the oven when cooked and golden. Slice each pizza into eight pieces and serve immediately, garnished with a dollop of sour cream.

Aussie

〜

A UNIQUELY AUSTRALIAN COMBINATION GARNISHED WITH TRADITIONAL
BREAKFAST OR LUNCHTIME FARE.

2 (8-ounce) dough balls (see page 8)

⅔ cup Pizza Sauce (see page 10)

1¼ cups grated mozzarella cheese

2 lamb cutlets (rib chops)

7 ounces tomatoes, roasted (see page 12)

5 ounces bacon, diced, cooked, and
drained

1 medium red onion, cut into wedges and
roasted (see page 12)

¼ bunch of lemon thyme leaves, chopped

2 eggs

freshly ground black pepper, to taste

MAKES 2 MEDIUM PIZZAS

Place two pizza stones or tiles in the oven. Heat the oven to 500°F. Roll out the pizza dough, as described on page 10, so that you have two bases. Cover the bases with the Pizza Sauce and mozzarella cheese, keeping a 1¼-inch border around the edge of the dough clean.

Cook the lamb cutlets in a small pan until they are just done. Set aside and keep warm.

Place the roast tomatoes on the bases in a random pattern, leaving spaces for other ingredients to fall into. Add the bacon and onion. Sprinkle the lemon thyme over the top.

Using a wide spatula or pizza paddle, gently slide each pizza onto a stone or tile. Cook for 10 minutes.

Meanwhile, fry the eggs in a nonstick frying pan or skillet. Set aside and keep warm.

Remove the pizzas from the oven when cooked and golden. Slice each pizza into eight pieces. Garnish each pizza with a fried egg and a lamb cutlet. Season with black pepper and serve immediately.

Salami with Goat Cheese & Pesto

~~~

BIG FLAVORS ROUNDED OUT WITH PESTO AND GOAT CHEESE MAKE FOR A CLASSIC COMBINATION OF PIZZA INGREDIENTS.

2 (8-ounce) dough balls (see page 8)

⅔ cup Pizza Sauce (see page 10)

1¼ cups grated mozzarella cheese

3 ounces salami, sliced

⅓ cup Pesto Sauce (see page 11)

1 red bell pepper, roasted and cut into chunks (see page 12)

2 tablespoons kalamata olives, pitted and cut into quarters

4 ounces goat cheese, cut into chunks

MAKES 2 MEDIUM PIZZAS

Place two pizza stones or tiles in the oven. Heat the oven to 500°F. Roll out the pizza dough, as described on page 10, so that you have two bases. Cover the bases with the Pizza Sauce and mozzarella cheese, keeping a 1¼-inch border around the edge of the dough clean.

Place the salami on the bases in a random pattern, leaving spaces for other ingredients to fall into. Using a teaspoon, place dollops of the Pesto Sauce on the pizzas. Add the red bell pepper, olives, and goat cheese.

Using a wide spatula or pizza paddle, gently slide each pizza onto a stone or tile. Cook for 10 minutes. Remove the pizzas from the oven when cooked and golden. Slice each pizza into eight pieces and serve immediately.

Grilled Lamb with Sweet Potato & Artichokes

~~~

THE CLASSIC INGREDIENTS LISTED HERE COULD WELL BE FROM A
TRADITIONAL BAKED DINNER INSTEAD OF A PIZZA. THE SAUTÉED
SWEET POTATO ADDS A NEW DIMENSION, BUT AN EXTREMELY TASTY ONE.

7 ounces lamb tenderloin, trimmed of
    any fat and sinew, then cut into pieces
    1½ inches long
salt and freshly ground black pepper,
    to taste
a little olive oil
2 (8-ounce) dough balls (see page 8)
⅔ cup Pizza Sauce (see page 10)
1¼ cups grated mozzarella cheese
2 medium red sweet potatoes, cut into
    slices, cooked then sautéed in a little
    olive oil with some rosemary
1 cup small oyster mushrooms, trimmed if
    necessary and rubbed with a little olive
    oil
2 marinated globe artichokes, quartered
4 teaspoons roast garlic purée (see page 13)
a few sprigs of rosemary
freshly ground black pepper, to taste

MAKES 2 MEDIUM PIZZAS

Flatten the lamb pieces with a meat tenderizer or pounder, until they are about ¼ inch thick. Season with salt and pepper. Heat a little olive oil in a frying pan or skillet until quite hot. Add the lamb and quickly sear on all sides to seal in the juices (just long enough to color the meat). Remove from the pan immediately. Set aside and allow to cool.

Place two pizza stones or tiles in the oven. Heat the oven to 500°F. Roll out the pizza dough, as described on page 10, so that you have two bases. Cover the bases with the Pizza Sauce and mozzarella cheese, keeping a 1¼-inch border around the edge of the dough clean.

Place the lamb on the bases in a random pattern, leaving spaces for other ingredients to fall into. Add the sweet potato, mushrooms, artichokes, and garlic. Sprinkle the rosemary over the top.

Using a wide spatula or pizza paddle, gently slide each pizza onto a stone or tile. Cook for 10 minutes. Remove from the oven when cooked and golden. Slice each pizza into eight pieces and serve immediately, seasoned with black pepper.

Supreme

~~~

THIS OLD STANDARD MAY BE A FIRM FAMILY FAVORITE, BUT WHEN MADE
WITH THE FRESHEST OF INGREDIENTS IT TAKES ON A WHOLE NEW
IDENTITY. THIS IS AN EXTREMELY EASY PIZZA TO OVERLOAD WITH TOPPING,
SO BE CAREFUL NOT TO STACK IT WITH TOO MANY LAYERS AS THIS
WILL PREVENT THE CHEESE UNDERNEATH FROM MELTING.

2 (8-ounce) dough balls (see page 8)

⅔ cup Pizza Sauce (see page 10)

1¼ cups grated mozzarella cheese

4 ounces spicy lamb sausage, cut into slices
¼ inch thick and seared in a frying pan
or skillet

4 ounces sliced double-smoked ham, cut
into small pieces

1 red bell pepper, diced

10–15 button mushrooms, sliced and
rubbed with a little olive oil

2 tablespoons kalamata olives, pitted and
cut into quarters

10 anchovy fillets, cut into pieces
(optional)

3–4 tablespoons grated mozzarella cheese
(extra)

MAKES 2 MEDIUM PIZZAS

Place two pizza stones or tiles in the oven.
Heat the oven to 500°F. Roll out the pizza
dough, as described on page 10, so that
you have two bases. Cover the bases with
the Pizza Sauce and mozzarella cheese,
keeping a 1¼-inch border around the edge
of the dough clean.

Place the sausage on the bases in a random pattern. Next add the ham, followed
by the red bell pepper, mushrooms, olives,
and anchovies (if using). Sprinkle the extra
mozzarella cheese over the top.

Using a wide spatula or pizza paddle,
gently slide each pizza onto a stone or tile.
Cook for 10 minutes. Remove the pizzas
from the oven when cooked and golden.
Slice each pizza into eight pieces and serve
immediately.

Super Supreme

〜〜〜

A HUGELY SATISFYING PIZZA FOR ALL TASTES AND AGES, FROM CHILDREN
TO ADULTS. FEEL FREE TO EXPERIMENT WITH EXTRA TOPPINGS TO SUIT
INDIVIDUAL TASTE, BUT BE CAREFUL NOT TO OVERLOAD THE PIZZA WITH
TOO MANY FLAVORS OR TOO MANY INGREDIENTS.

2 (8-ounce) dough balls (see page 8)
⅔ cup Pizza Sauce (see page 10)
1¼ cups grated mozzarella cheese
1½ ounces pepperoni, sliced
1½ ounces salami, sliced
3 ounces fresh sausage, cut into slices
 ¼ inch thick and seared in a frying pan
 or skillet
4 tomatoes, roasted (see page 12) and cut
 into quarters
1 red onion, thinly sliced into rings
10 button mushrooms, sliced and rubbed
 with a little olive oil
2 tablespoons green olives, pitted and cut
 into quarters
2 teaspoons roast garlic purée (see page 13)

MAKES 2 MEDIUM PIZZAS

Place two pizza stones or tiles in the oven.
Heat the oven to 500°F. Roll out the pizza
dough, as described on page 10, so that
you have two bases. Cover the bases with
the Pizza Sauce and mozzarella cheese,
keeping a 1¼-inch border around the edge
of the dough clean.

Place the pepperoni, salami, and sausage
on the bases in a random pattern, leaving
spaces for other ingredients to fall into. Be
careful not to stack too many ingredients on
top of each other. Add the roast tomatoes,
onion rings, mushrooms, and olives. Dot the
roast garlic over the top. You may like to
sprinkle a little extra mozzarella cheese over
the top to hold the ingredients together.

Using a wide spatula or pizza paddle,
gently slide each pizza onto a stone or tile.
Cook for 10 minutes. Remove the pizzas
from the oven when cooked and golden.
Slice each pizza into eight pieces and serve
immediately.

Sausage with Cherry Tomatoes, Bacon, & Mushrooms

~~~

SHOULD YOU FEEL LIKE A PIZZA FOR BREAKFAST, THIS IS TYPICAL
MORNING FARE WITH A TWIST. THIS HEARTY TOPPING IS GUARANTEED
TO GET YOUR ENGINE RUNNING!

2 (8-ounce) dough balls (see page 8)

⅔ cup Pizza Sauce (see page 10)

1¼ cups grated mozzarella cheese

7 ounces fresh sausage of your choice, cut into slices ¼-inch thick and seared in a frying pan or skillet

4 ounces bacon slices, diced and cooked

½ pint cherry tomatoes, halved

12 button mushrooms, sliced and lightly oiled

3 scallions, sliced on the angle, Chinese style

MAKES 2 MEDIUM PIZZAS

Place two pizza stones or tiles in the oven. Heat the oven to 500°F. Roll out the pizza dough, as described on page 10, so that you have two bases. Cover the bases with the Pizza Sauce and mozzarella cheese, keeping a 1¼-inch border around the edge of the dough clean.

Place the sausage on the bases in a random pattern, leaving spaces for other ingredients to fall into. Add the bacon, cherry tomatoes, mushrooms, and scallions. Sprinkle a little extra mozzarella cheese over the top if desired.

Using a wide spatula or pizza paddle, gently slide each pizza onto a stone or tile. Cook for 10 minutes. Remove the pizzas from the oven when cooked and golden. Slice each pizza into eight pieces and serve immediately.

Tex Mex

~~~

GROUND BEEF WITH PINTO BEANS IN A MILD TOMATO SAUCE MAKE THIS
A TASTY PIZZA, ESPECIALLY WHEN ENHANCED WITH SOUR CREAM AND
GUACAMOLE. A SIMPLE RECIPE FOR GUACAMOLE IS PROVIDED, BUT IF
TIME IS AGAINST YOU, THERE ARE MANY READY-MADE AVOCADO DIPS
AVAILABLE FROM YOUR SUPERMARKET.

GUACAMOLE

2 avocados
½ red onion, diced
¼ bunch of coriander (cilantro), leaves
   picked and chopped
¼ teaspoon chile paste, or to taste
juice of ½ lemon
juice of ½ lime
salt and freshly ground black pepper,
   to taste

TEX MEX SAUCE

4 teaspoons olive oil
1 onion, finely diced
1 green bell pepper, finely diced
1 teaspoon chile paste
1 teaspoon crushed garlic
11 ounces ground beef
1 can (14 ounces) crushed tomatoes
¼ cup Barbecue Sauce (see page 11)
4 teaspoons tomato paste
1 can (5 ounces) cooked pinto beans
salt and freshly ground black pepper, to
   taste

PIZZA

2 (8-ounce) dough balls (see page 8)
Tex Mex Sauce
1¼ cups grated mozzarella cheese
½ medium red onion, thinly sliced into
   rings
½ cup sour cream
½ cup Guacamole
large handful of corn chips

MAKES 2 MEDIUM PIZZAS

GUACAMOLE

Halve and pit the avocados. Peel and cut the
flesh into large pieces. Place in a bowl and
add the remaining ingredients. Mix thoroughly until smooth. Store covered in the
refrigerator until needed.

TEX MEX SAUCE

Heat the olive oil in a medium saucepan. Add the onion, bell pepper, chile paste, and garlic. Sauté until the onion is transparent. Add the beef, breaking it up with a wooden spoon as it browns so that it does not become lumpy. Simmer for 20 minutes.

Add the tomatoes, Barbecue Sauce, and tomato paste. Simmer for another 10 minutes before adding the beans. Return to the boil and season with salt and pepper. Remove from the heat and allow to cool before using. The mixture will thicken to a heavy paste.

Place two pizza stones or tiles in the oven. Heat the oven to 500°F. Roll out the pizza dough, as described on page 10, so that you have two bases.

Spoon the Tex Mex Sauce onto the bases, keeping a 1¼-inch border around the edge of the dough clean. Sprinkle the mozzarella cheese over the top. Place the onion rings over each pizza in a random pattern.

Using a wide spatula or pizza paddle, gently slide each pizza onto a stone or tile. Cook for 10 minutes. Remove the pizzas from the oven when cooked and golden. Slice each pizza into eight pieces. Place a dollop each of sour cream and Guacamole in the center of each pizza. Stand a few corn chips in the center of each pizza. Serve immediately.

Ham, Broccoli, & Almonds with Dijon Mustard

~~~

THE BASE SAUCE FOR THIS PIZZA IS MADE WITH MASCARPONE CHEESE AND
DIJON MUSTARD. THE FLAVORS REMAIN SUBTLE, YET COMPLEMENT
THE OTHER INGREDIENTS PERFECTLY.

2 (8-ounce) dough balls (see page 8)
1¼ cup (5 ounces) mascarpone cheese
¼ cup Dijon mustard
1¼ cups grated mozzarella cheese
2 heads broccoli, cut into florets and
  blanched
7 ounces sliced double-smoked ham, cut
  into strips ¼ inch wide and 1¼ inches long
1½ ounces Brie cheese, cut into slices
  ¼ inch thick
2–3 tablespoons sliced almonds

MAKES 2 MEDIUM PIZZAS

Place two pizza stones or tiles in the oven. Heat the oven to 500°F. Roll out the pizza dough, as described on page 10, so that you have two bases. Thoroughly combine the mascarpone cheese and Dijon mustard. Use this mixture to cover the bases, then sprinkle the mozzarella cheese over the top, keeping a 1¼-inch border from the edge of the dough clean.

Place the broccoli on the bases in a random pattern, leaving spaces for other ingredients to fall into. Add the ham. Break the slices of Brie into pieces 1¼ inches long and place on the pizza. Sprinkle the sliced almonds over the top.

Using a wide spatula or pizza paddle, gently slide each pizza onto a stone or tile. Cook for 10 minutes. Remove the pizzas from the oven when cooked and golden. Slice each pizza into eight pieces and serve immediately.

Market
CUISINE

THIS ASSORTMENT OF PIZZAS SHOWS YOU HOW TO MAKE
THE MOST OF SEASONALLY AVAILABLE PRODUCE AND
THE FRESHEST OF INGREDIENTS.

IN ESSENCE, THE BASE IS COOKED SEPARATELY WITH
ONLY SOME OF THE INGREDIENTS ON THE TOPPING.
MEANWHILE, THE MARKET CUISINE IS GRILLED, PAN-FRIED
OR ROASTED BEFORE BEING PLACED ON THE PIZZA AT THE
LAST MINUTE. AFTER GARNISHING ACCORDINGLY, THE
PIZZA IS BROUGHT TO THE TABLE IMMEDIATELY.

THIS METHOD OF ASSEMBLY IS VERY SIMILAR IN STYLE TO
PRODUCING AN À LA CARTE MEAL, BUT HERE THE PIZZA BASE
IS USED AS THE VEHICLE ON WHICH TO SERVE THE FOOD.

MOST OF THESE "MARKET CUISINE" PIZZAS ARE BEST MADE
AS INDIVIDUAL SERVINGS, USING THE SAME SIZE DOUGH
BALL AS FOR THE MEDIUM PIZZAS, BUT TRIMMED TO A
DIAMETER OF 7 INCHES.

Roast Flounder, Peppers, Bermuda Onions, & Hazelnut Coriander Pesto

~~~

A MAGNIFICENT PIZZA OF JUST-COOKED FISH WITH PESTO DRIZZLED OVER
THE TOP. THE FLOUNDER CAN BE REPLACED WITH ANY FIRM-FLESHED
WHITE FISH. ALTHOUGH THE PESTO WILL LAST IN THE REFRIGERATOR
FOR SOME TIME, IT IS BEST USED AS QUICKLY AS POSSIBLE AS
THE DELICATE CORIANDER BOUQUET DETERIORATES RAPIDLY.

HAZELNUT CORIANDER PESTO
⅔ cup (about 2 handfuls) coriander
   (cilantro) leaves
¼ cup (about 1 small handful) chopped
   chives
4 teaspoons shelled and roasted hazelnuts
1 clove garlic
2 tablespoons olive oil
4 teaspoons grated Parmesan cheese

PIZZA
2 (8-ounce) dough balls (see page 8)
⅓ cup Pizza Sauce (see page 10)
¾ cup grated mozzarella cheese
1 red bell pepper, roasted, peeled, and
   diced (see page 12)
1 Bermuda or red onion, cut into wedges
   and roasted (see page 12)

a little olive oil
4 medium flounder fillets (about 14
   ounces), skinned and boned

MAKES 2 INDIVIDUAL PIZZAS

HAZELNUT CORIANDER PESTO
Put the coriander, chives, hazelnuts, and
garlic in an electric blender or food processor. Blend or process until finely chopped.
With the motor running, slowly add the oil
and Parmesan cheese. Blend into a smooth
purée. Transfer to a bowl, cover, and set
aside until needed. (If you are not making
your pizza immediately, refrigerate the pesto
until needed.)

Place two pizza stones or tiles in the oven. Heat the oven to 500°F. Roll out the pizza dough, as described on page 10, so that you have two bases. Find a plate approximately 7 inches in diameter and place it face down on one of the bases. Take a sharp knife and run it around the outside of the plate to cut a smaller base. Remove the plate. You should now have a round, smooth-edged base. Repeat with the other base.

Cover the bases with the Pizza Sauce and mozzarella cheese, keeping a ½-inch border around the edge of the dough clean. Place the red bell pepper and onion on the bases in a random pattern.

Using a wide spatula or pizza paddle, gently slide each pizza onto a stone or tile. Cook for 8 minutes.

Meanwhile, heat a little olive oil in a non-stick frying pan or skillet over a moderate heat. When the oil is shimmering, add the fish to the pan. Let it start to color and then turn. Continue cooking until the other side has started to color. Remove from the pan. Your pizzas should be ready now.

Remove the pizzas from the oven when cooked and golden. Slice each pizza into four pieces. Place the pizzas on serving plates before assembling. Add the fish pieces in a random pattern. Drizzle the pesto all over the pizzas and serve immediately.

Pancetta, Asparagus, Spinach, & Poached Egg

ADDING A SOFT POACHED EGG ALMOST TURNS THIS PIZZA INTO BREAKFAST FARE.
THE SPINACH IS RAW WHEN PLACED ON THE TOPPING, BUT THE COMBINED
HEAT OF THE PIZZA AND THE POACHED EGG MEANS THAT IT QUICKLY COOKS.

1 bunch of asparagus
2 (8-ounce) dough balls (see page 8)
⅓ cup Pizza Sauce (see page 10)
¾ cup grated mozzarella cheese
¾ ounce sliced pancetta
2 eggs
12–15 baby spinach leaves, rinsed and
   stems removed
freshly ground black pepper, to taste

MAKES 2 INDIVIDUAL PIZZAS

Peel the bottom two thirds of the stems of the asparagus. Steam or poach the spears in hot water for 2–3 minutes until just done. Plunge into icy cold water to stop the asparagus cooking any further. Drain when cool. Cut the thicker stems in half lengthways and trim the spears into pieces about 2 inches long. Set aside.

Place two pizza stones or tiles in the oven. Heat the oven to 500°F. Roll out the pizza dough, as described on page 10, so that you have two bases. Find a plate approximately 7 inches in diameter and place it face down on one of the bases. Take a sharp knife and run it around the outside of the plate to cut a smaller base. Remove the plate. You should now have a round, smooth-edged base. Repeat with the other base.

Cover the bases with the Pizza Sauce and mozzarella cheese, keeping a ½-inch border around the edge of the dough clean. Place the asparagus spears on the bases in a clock-style pattern, with the spears pointing outward from the center of each pizza. Add the pancetta, allowing one piece per slice and one for the middle of each pizza.

Using a wide spatula or pizza paddle, gently slide each pizza onto a stone or tile. Cook for 8 minutes. Meanwhile, gently poach the eggs for 3–4 minutes. Remove the pizzas from the oven when cooked and golden. Slice each pizza into four pieces. Place the pizzas on serving plates before assembling. Put a small pile of spinach leaves in the center of each pizza. Top with a poached egg. Garnish with black pepper and serve immediately.

Niçoise Pizza with Tuna

~~~

A FABULOUS PIZZA THAT IS ESPECIALLY DELICIOUS WHEN SERVED
IN THE WARMER MONTHS OF THE YEAR WHEN TUNA, GREEN BEANS, AND
TOMATOES REACH THEIR SEASONAL PEAK.

2 (8-ounce) dough balls (see page 8)
⅓ cup Pizza Sauce (see page 10)
¾ cup grated mozzarella cheese
8 kalamata olives, pitted and halved
1 medium potato, peeled and boiled
4 cherry tomatoes, halved
1½ ounces feta cheese, diced
8 ounces tuna fillet or steaks
salt and freshly ground black pepper,
    to taste
2 ounces green beans, blanched and cut
    into 1¼-inch pieces
juice of ½ lemon

MAKES 2 INDIVIDUAL PIZZAS

Place two pizza stones or tiles in the oven. Heat the oven to 500°F. Roll out the pizza dough, as described on page 10, so that you have two bases. Find a plate approximately 7 inches in diameter and place it face down on one of the bases. Take a sharp knife and run it around the outside of the plate to cut a smaller base. Remove the plate. You should now have a round, smooth-edged base. Repeat with the other base.

Cover the bases with the Pizza Sauce and mozzarella cheese, keeping a ½-inch border around the edge of the dough clean. Place the olives on the bases in a random pattern. Cut the potato into quarters and slice. Add to the bases with the cherry tomatoes and feta cheese. Using a wide spatula or pizza paddle, gently slide each pizza onto a stone or tile. Cook for 8 minutes.

Meanwhile, place the tuna on a lightly oiled tray and season with salt and pepper. Broil or barbecue by quickly searing on both sides. (Alternatively, quickly sear on both sides in a frying pan or skillet.) Carefully slice the tuna into strips ¼ inch wide. Place the tuna and green beans on a plate and drizzle with the lemon juice. Your pizzas should be ready now.

Remove the pizzas from the oven when cooked and golden. Slice each pizza into four pieces. Place the pizzas on serving plates before assembling. Spoon the tuna and beans over the pizzas. Drizzle with any leftover lemon juice and serve immediately.

Togarashi Beef

~~~

FOR THIS HOT AND SPICY JAPANESE-SEASONED PIZZA, THE BEEF IS
COATED IN TOGARASHI SEASONING AND THEN WOK-CHARRED.

8 ounces beef rump or sirloin, cut into
small strips about 1¼ inches × ½ inch

2 teaspoons togarashi seasoning (available
from Asian or gourmet stores)

4 large cap or field mushrooms, peeled
if necessary and cut into slices ½ inch
thick

2 (8-ounce) dough balls (see page 8)

⅓ cup Pizza Sauce (see page 10)

¾ cup grated mozzarella cheese

2 scallions, finely sliced

a little sesame oil

1 small carrot, cut into very fine julienne
about 1¼ inches long

a few coriander (cilantro) leaves,
to garnish

MAKES 2 INDIVIDUAL PIZZAS

Marinate the beef in the togarashi seasoning
for at least 2 hours.

Grill or barbecue the mushrooms until
they start to color. Turn and cook on the
other side. Alternatively, sauté in a little butter in a frying pan or skillet. Remove from
the pan and drain. Set aside.

Place two pizza stones or tiles in the
oven. Heat the oven to 500°F. Roll out the
pizza dough, as described on page 10,
so that you have two bases. Find a plate
approximately 7 inches in diameter and
place it face down on one of the bases.
Take a sharp knife and run it around the
outside of the plate to cut a smaller base.
Remove the plate. You should now have a
round, smooth-edged base. Repeat with the
other base.

Cover the bases with the Pizza Sauce and
mozzarella cheese, keeping a ½-inch border
around the edge of the dough clean. Place
the mushrooms on the bases. Sprinkle the
scallions over the top. Using a wide spatula
or pizza paddle, gently slide each pizza
onto a stone or tile. Cook for 8 minutes.

Halfway through the cooking time, heat
the sesame oil in a wok or frying pan over
a high heat. When the oil is almost smoking,
add the beef and carrot. Stir-fry for about
2 minutes, to seal the meat. Remove from
the wok and drain.

Remove the pizzas from the oven when
cooked and golden. Slice each pizza into
four pieces. Place on serving plates before
assembling. Spoon the beef and carrot onto
the pizzas. Garnish with the coriander and
serve immediately.

Grilled Shrimp, Roma Tomatoes, & Oregano Pesto

FRESH SHRIMP COMPLEMENTED WITH FLAVORS TYPICAL OF TUSCANY
SEEM TO MAKE THIS PIZZA ALMOST IRRESISTIBLE.

OREGANO PESTO

2 large red bell peppers, roasted, peeled
  and seeded (see page 12)
¼ cup pine nuts, toasted
3 large cloves garlic, roasted and peeled
  (see page 13)
large handful of oregano, freshly
  chopped
¼ cup extra-virgin olive oil
¼ cup Parmesan cheese shavings

PIZZA

2 (8-ounce) dough balls (see page 8)
⅔ cup Pizza Sauce (see page 10)
1¼ cups grated mozzarella cheese
8 small Roma (plum) tomatoes, halved and
  roasted (see page 12)
1 large bell pepper, roasted, peeled, seeded
  and cut into chunks (see page 12)
a few oregano leaves, freshly chopped
16 fresh shrimp, peeled, deveined, and cut
  in half lengthwise

MAKES 2 MEDIUM PIZZAS

OREGANO PESTO

Blend or process the roast red bell pepper, pine nuts, roast garlic, and oregano until finely chopped. Add the olive oil and Parmesan cheese. Blend until smooth.

Place two pizza stones or tiles in the oven. Heat the oven to 500°F. Roll out the dough, as described on page 10, so that you have two bases. Cover with the Pizza Sauce and mozzarella cheese, keeping a 1¼-inch border around the edge of the dough clean.
  Place the roast tomato and roast bell pepper on each of the bases. Sprinkle the oregano over the top. Using a wide spatula or pizza paddle, gently slide each pizza onto a stone or tile. Cook for 10 minutes. Meanwhile, lightly broil or barbecue the shellfish on both sides. Remove the pizzas from the oven when cooked and golden. Slice each pizza into eight pieces and place a shellfish on each slice. Spoon the Oregano Pesto over the top and serve immediately.

Open Souvlaki

THIS PIZZA WAS THE PIONEER OF ALL OUR MARKET CUISINE CREATIONS
AND IT STILL HAS A HIGH FOLLOWING AMONG OUR LUNCHTIME CLIENTELE.
THE BEST WAY TO COOK THE LAMB IS ON THE BARS OF A VERY HOT BARBECUE
OR BROILER. IF YOU DON'T HAVE EITHER OF THESE, USE A VERY HOT
FRYING PAN OR SKILLET, AND SIMPLY SEAR THE MEAT ON EACH SIDE.

1 loin of lamb, about 12 ounces, trimmed
  of any fat and skin
a little olive oil
2 cloves garlic, crushed
2 (8-ounce) dough balls (see page 8)
⅓ cup Pizza Sauce (see page 10)
¾ cup grated mozzarella cheese
1 red bell pepper, roasted, peeled, seeded
  and cut into dice (see page 12)
3 ounces herb and garlic cream cheese, cut
  into large chunks
2 handfuls baby mixed leaves or mesclun,
  rinsed and dried
¼ cup tabbouleh (see next page)
a little balsamic vinegar
a little olive oil
freshly ground black pepper, to taste

MAKES 2 INDIVIDUAL PIZZAS

Cut the lamb into slices ½ inch thick. You
should have 10–12 slices. Tenderize the
lamb with a meat hammer. Marinate in
a little olive oil with the crushed garlic.

Place two pizza stones or tiles in the
oven. Heat the oven to 500°F. Roll out the
pizza dough, as described on page 10,
so that you have two bases. Find a plate
approximately 7 inches in diameter and
place it face down on one of the bases.
Take a sharp knife and run it around the
outside of the plate to cut a smaller base.
Remove the plate. You should now have a
round, smooth-edged base. Repeat with the
other base.

Cover the bases with the Pizza Sauce and
mozzarella cheese, keeping a ½-inch border
around the edge of the dough clean. Place
the red bell pepper and cream cheese on the
bases in a random pattern.

Using a wide spatula or pizza paddle,
gently slide each pizza onto a stone or tile.
Cook for 8 minutes.

Meanwhile, quickly sear the lamb slices
on both sides on the bars of a very hot barbecue (use a very hot frying pan or skillet if

you do not have a barbecue). Do not over-cook the lamb; simply seal the meat on each side. Your pizzas should be ready now.

Remove the pizzas from the oven when cooked and golden. Slice each pizza into four pieces. Place the pizzas on serving plates before assembling. Lay the lamb slices around the border of the topping, with one slice in the middle. Place a small pile of mixed leaves or mesclun in the center of each pizza (on top of the lamb). Spoon the tabbouleh over the top of the mixed leaves. Drizzle each pizza with a few drops of bal-samic vinegar and a little olive oil. Season with black pepper and serve immediately.

TABBOULEH

Cut 1 tomato into wedges and discard the seeds. Cut the tomato flesh into dice. Combine the tomato with 1 tablespoon cooked couscous and 1 tablespoon chopped flat-leaf (Italian) parsley. Set aside until ready to use.

If you do not have the time to prepare your own tabbouleh for this pizza, you can use a good-quality store-bought one instead.

Baby Octopus, Eggplant, Roast Peppers, & Sweet Basil Oil

THIS PIZZA FEATURES BABY OCTOPUS, PILED HIGH ON A NEST OF MEDITERRANEAN VEGETABLES, AND THEN DRIZZLED WITH A FRUITY, BASIL-INFUSED OLIVE OIL. THE OCTOPUS SHOULD BE CHARRED ON A BARBECUE TO BRING OUT THE BEST FLAVOR.

SWEET BASIL OIL

½ large bunch of basil
2 whole cloves garlic, roasted (see page 13)
1 cup extra-virgin olive oil
1 cup pure olive oil

BABY OCTOPUS

11 ounces baby octopus, beak and eyes removed, trimmed and cleaned
grated peel and juice of 1 lemon
1 tablespoon olive oil
salt and freshly ground black pepper, to taste

PIZZA

2 (8-ounce) dough balls (see page 8)
⅔ cup Pizza Sauce (see page 10)
1¼ cups grated mozzarella cheese
1 large eggplant, cut into slices ¼ inch thick, roasted (see page 103)

1 large red bell pepper, roasted, peeled and cut into chunks (see page 12)
2 scallions, sliced on the angle, Chinese style
1 tablespoon Sweet Basil Oil (see opposite) or extra virgin olive oil

MAKES 2 MEDIUM PIZZAS

SWEET BASIL OIL

Place the basil, roast garlic, extra-virgin olive oil, and pure olive oil in a jar. Make sure that the basil is completely submerged, otherwise it may become moldy. Seal the jar and let stand in a cool, dark place for at least 1 week before using. This oil will last indefinitely if stored in the refrigerator.

Place the baby octopus in a shallow container. Add the lemon peel and juice, and the olive oil. Season with salt and pepper. Leave to marinate while preparing the rest of the pizza.

Place two pizza stones or tiles in the oven. Heat the oven to 500°F. Roll out the pizza dough, as described on page 10, so that you have two bases. Cover the bases with the Pizza Sauce and mozzarella cheese, keeping a 1¼-inch border around the edge of the dough clean.

Cut the roast eggplant into chunks. Place on each of the bases in a random pattern. Add the roast red bell pepper. Sprinkle the scallions over the top. Using a wide spatula or pizza paddle, gently slide each pizza onto a stone or tile. Cook for 10 minutes.

Meanwhile, sear the baby octopus on a barbecue or broiler. Allow to char lightly and the ends to become crisp before turning to cook on the other side.

Remove the pizzas from the oven when cooked and golden. Slice each pizza into eight pieces. Pile the baby octopus in the center of each pizza. Drizzle with the Sweet Basil Oil and serve immediately.

Duck Sausage, Pistachios, Sweet Potato, & Sage

~~~

A SPECIALIZED BUTCHER WILL STOCK THE SAUSAGES NEEDED FOR
THIS PIZZA, BUT FEEL FREE TO REPLACE THEM WITH ANOTHER VARIETY,
SUCH AS COTECHINO, LOUKANIKA, OR CHORIZO.

4 medium to large duck or other fresh
  sausages
2 (8-ounce) dough balls (see page 8)
⅔ cup Pizza Sauce (see page 10)
1½ cups grated mozzarella cheese
1 medium sweet potato, cut into slices
  ¼ inch thick and roasted (see page 103)
1 medium red onion, cut into wedges and
  roasted (see page 12)
2 teaspoons chopped pistachio nuts
a few fresh sage leaves, freshly chopped
  (do not chop the leaves until you are
  ready to use them or they will lose their
  fragrance and flavor)

MAKES 2 MEDIUM PIZZAS

Blanch the sausages in boiling water for
several minutes. Sauté in a frying pan or
skillet over a medium heat for 8–10 minutes.
Allow to cool. Cut into slices ½ inch thick.
Set aside.

Place two pizza stones or tiles in the
oven. Heat the oven to 500°F. Roll out the
pizza dough, as described on page 10, so
that you have two bases. Cover the bases
with the Pizza Sauce and 1⅓ cups of the
mozzarella cheese, keeping a 1¼-inch border around the edge of the dough clean.

Place the sausage on each of the bases
in a random pattern. Add the sweet potato,
roast onion, and pistachio nuts. Scatter the
remaining mozzarella cheese over the pizzas. Sprinkle the sage over the top.

Using a wide spatula or pizza paddle,
gently slide each pizza onto a stone or tile.
Cook for 10 minutes. Remove the pizzas
from the oven when cooked and golden.
Slice each pizza into eight pieces and serve
immediately.

Primavera

~~~

THIS IS A VERY SIMPLE PIZZA BASED ON AN ITALIAN PRIMAVERA
OR SPRING PIE. ASPARAGUS, FRESH PEAS, GREEN BEANS, AND CHERRY
TOMATOES—ALL PLENTIFUL IN THE MARKETS WHEN THEY ARE IN SEASON—
ARE COMPLEMENTED BY ROMANO CHEESE.

¾ cup shelled fresh green peas
⅔ cup fine green beans
12 spears young asparagus
2 (8-ounce) dough balls (see page 8)
⅔ cup Pizza Sauce (see page 10)
1¼ cups grated mozzarella cheese
10 cherry tomatoes, halved
½ cup freshly shaved Romano cheese
½ small handful of basil leaves, freshly
    chopped
freshly ground black pepper, to taste

MAKES 2 MEDIUM PIZZAS

Blanch the peas, green beans, and asparagus in separate small saucepans of boiling water until just cooked. Be careful not to overcook the vegetables as they must retain their crispness and vibrant colors. Refresh in icy cold water. Allow to drain. Cut the green beans and asparagus into 1¼-inch lengths.

Place two pizza stones or tiles in the oven. Heat the oven to 500°F. Roll out the pizza dough, as described on page 10, so that you have two bases. Cover the bases with the Pizza Sauce and mozzarella cheese, keeping a 1¼-inch border around the edge of the dough clean.

Place the cherry tomatoes on each of the bases in a random pattern. Spoon the peas over the top. Add the green beans and asparagus. Scatter the Romano cheese over the pizzas and sprinkle with the basil.

Using a wide spatula or pizza paddle, gently slide each pizza onto a stone or tile. Cook for 10 minutes. Remove the pizzas from the oven when cooked and golden. Slice each pizza into eight pieces and serve immediately, seasoned with the black pepper.

Smoked Trout, Bok Choy, & Enoki Mushrooms

〜〜〜

A DELICATELY FLAVORED PIZZA WITH SUBTLE TASTES THAT MELD TO FORM A UNIQUE EAST–WEST COMBINATION.

1 bunch of bok choy (Chinese white cabbage)

1 scallion, finely sliced

2 teaspoons grated ginger

5 ounces smoked trout, sliced and cut into strips about ½ inch wide

2 teaspoons soy sauce

freshly ground black pepper, to taste

2 (8-ounce) dough balls (see page 8)

⅓ cup Pizza Sauce (see page 10)

¾ cup grated mozzarella cheese

8 pear tomatoes, halved

a little olive oil

8 ounces enoki mushrooms, stems discarded

4 basil leaves, sliced

½ teaspoon sesame seeds

MAKES 2 INDIVIDUAL PIZZAS

Blanch the bok choy in boiling water until just cooked. Refresh in icy cold water. Pat dry and slice into fine strips. Place the bok choy, scallion, ginger, smoked trout, and soy sauce in a bowl. Mix thoroughly. Season with pepper.

Place two pizza stones or tiles in the oven. Heat the oven to 500°F. Roll out the pizza dough, as described on page 10, so that you have two bases. Find a plate approximately 7 inches in diameter and place it face down on one of the bases. Take a sharp knife and run it around the outside of the plate to cut a smaller base. Remove the plate. You should now have a round, smooth-edged base. Repeat with the other base.

Cover the bases with the Pizza Sauce and mozzarella cheese, keeping a ½-inch border around the edge of the dough clean. Place a thin layer of the bok choy mixture over the top. Add the pear tomatoes. Using a wide spatula or pizza paddle, gently slide each pizza onto a stone or tile. Cook for 8 minutes.

Meanwhile, heat a little olive oil in a frying pan or skillet. Add the mushrooms. Sauté for 2–3 minutes. Stir the basil and sesame seeds through the mushrooms.

Remove the pizzas from the oven when cooked and golden. Slice each pizza into four pieces. Place the pizzas on serving plates. Spoon the mushrooms over the top and serve immediately.

Fruits of the
SEA

WITH SUCH AN ARRAY OF PLENTIFUL MORSELS
TO CHOOSE FROM, WITH OR WITHOUT SHELLS, SEAFOOD
MAKES A SUPERB PIZZA TOPPING. THE FLAVORS OF
SEAFOOD ARE DELICATE AND THE MEAT IS SWEET.
PARTNERED INGREDIENTS SHOULD ALWAYS BE POLITE
IN TASTE, COMPLEMENTING RATHER THAN DROWNING
OUT SEAFOOD'S SUBTLE FLAVORS.

ALWAYS SELECT THE FRESHEST FISH AND SHELLFISH.
COOK IT QUICKLY TO SEAL IN THE JUICES. STIR-FRYING,
BARBECUING, AND STEAMING—ALL FAST METHODS OF
COOKING—ARE THE MOST SUITABLE. MOST IMPORTANTLY,
NEVER OVERCOOK SEAFOOD.

Tuscan

~~~

THIS PIZZA COMBINES THE FLAVORS OF SELECT SEAFOOD WITH THOSE OF TOMATO, GARLIC, AND BASIL TO PRODUCE THE TASTE OF TUSCANY.

2 (8-ounce) dough balls (see page 8)
⅔ cup Pizza Sauce (see page 10)
1¾ cups grated mozzarella cheese
3 ounces mussels, cooked (see page 6)
12 shrimp, cooked, peeled, and deveined
3 ounces scallops, cooked (see page 6)
4 small to medium tomatoes, roasted
   (see page 12)
3 tablespoons roast garlic purée
   (see page 13)
½ bunch of basil, finely sliced
freshly ground black pepper, to taste

MAKES 2 MEDIUM PIZZAS

Place two pizza stones or tiles in the oven. Heat the oven to 500°F. Roll out the pizza dough, as described on page 10, so that you have two bases. Cover the bases with the Pizza Sauce and mozzarella cheese (reserve some cheese for topping the pizza), keeping a 1¼-inch border around the edge of the dough clean.

Distribute the seafood evenly over each base in a clock-style pattern, placing the mussels, shrimp, and scallops alternately. Place any leftover seafood in the center of the pizza in a similar pattern. Add the tomatoes and dollops of the roast garlic, placing all over the pizzas. Sprinkle the extra cheese and the basil over the top.

Using a wide spatula or pizza paddle, gently slide each pizza onto a stone or tile. Cook for 10 minutes. Remove the pizzas from the oven when cooked and golden. Slice each pizza into eight pieces and serve immediately, garnished with the black pepper.

Cajun Scallops

~~~

YOU WILL NEED CAJUN SEASONING FOR THIS SOUTHERN-STYLE PIZZA.
YOU MAY BE ABLE TO BUY THIS, BUT I HAVE GIVEN A SIMPLE RECIPE FOR
MAKING YOUR OWN. ONCE YOU HAVE, IT WILL LAST INDEFINITELY.

2 (8-ounce) dough balls (see page 8)
⅔ cup Pizza Sauce (see page 10)
1¼ cups grated mozzarella cheese
8 ounces scallops, dusted in Cajun season-
    ing and seared on both sides in a very
    hot pan (see page 6 for notes on cooking
    seafood)
5 ounces red sweet potato, cut into slices
    ¼ inch thick and roasted in a moderate
    oven at 325°F for 12–15 minutes or
    until cooked
1 medium red onion, cut into wedges and
    roasted (see page 12)
1 red bell pepper, roasted and cut into
    chunks (see page 12)
½ bunch of chives, finely sliced

CAJUN SEASONING
3 tablespoons paprika
pinch of cayenne (red) pepper
1 teaspoon garlic powder
1 teaspoon ground white pepper

MAKES 2 MEDIUM PIZZAS

Place two pizza stones or tiles in the oven. Heat the oven to 500°F. Roll out the pizza dough, as described on page 10, so that you have two bases. Cover the bases with the Pizza Sauce and mozzarella cheese, keeping a 1¼-inch border around the edge of the dough clean.

Distribute the scallops evenly over each base in a clock-style pattern. Place any left-over scallops in the center of each pizza in a similar pattern. Add the sweet potato, onion, and bell pepper.

Using a wide spatula or pizza paddle, gently slide each pizza onto a stone or tile. Cook for 10 minutes. Remove the pizzas from the oven when cooked and golden. Slice each pizza into eight pieces and serve immediately, garnished with the chives.

CAJUN SEASONING
Combine the paprika, cayenne pepper, garlic powder, and ground white pepper in a bowl. Mix thoroughly.

This seasoning will last indefinitely if stored in an airtight container.

Creole Seafood with Roast Peppers & Lemon Chile Oil

~~~

THIS PIZZA IS FINISHED WITH A LEMON CHILE OIL THAT IS ESPECIALLY FIERY. BE CONSERVATIVE WITH THE AMOUNT YOU POUR ON UNTIL YOU DISCOVER EXACTLY HOW HOT THIS OIL IS.

LEMON CHILE OIL

scant ½ cup peanut oil
2 teaspoons sesame oil
4 teaspoons red chile powder
½ teaspoon black peppercorns
½ teaspoon crushed garlic
1½ teaspoons chopped fresh ginger
½ teaspoon chopped dried lemon grass
grated peel of 1 lemon

PIZZA

2 (8-ounce) dough balls (see page 8)
⅔ cup Pizza Sauce (see page 10)
1¼ cups grated mozzarella cheese
3 ounces scallops, cooked (see page 6)
5 ounces lobster meat, cooked
   (see page 6)
2 ounces mussels, cooked (see page 6)
4 scallions, sliced on the angle, Chinese
   style

1 red bell pepper, roasted, peeled, and cut
   into chunks (see page 12)
coriander (cilantro) leaves, to garnish
   (optional)

MAKES 2 MEDIUM PIZZAS

LEMON CHILE OIL

Combine the peanut and sesame oils in a small saucepan. Place over a gentle heat until the oil mixture starts to shimmer. Be extremely careful, as the oil may splutter.

Place the chilli powder, black peppercorns, garlic, ginger, and lemon grass in a stainless steel bowl. Carefully pour the shimmering oil over the top and let stand for 3 minutes.

Add the lemon peel and let the oil stand for at least 24 hours before using.

This oil will keep indefinitely if stored in an airtight jar or bottle in a cool, dark place.

Place two pizza stones or tiles in the oven. Heat the oven to 500°F. Roll out the pizza dough, as described on page 10, so that you have two bases. Cover the bases with the Pizza Sauce and mozzarella cheese, keeping a 1¼-inch border around the edge of the dough clean.

Distribute the seafood evenly over each base in a clock-style pattern, placing the scallops, lobster meat, and mussels alternately. Place any leftover seafood in the center of the pizza in a similar pattern. Add the scallions and roasted bell pepper.

Using a wide spatula or pizza paddle, gently slide each pizza onto a stone or tile. Cook for 10 minutes. Remove the pizzas from the oven when cooked and golden. Slice each pizza into eight pieces and drizzle a little of the Lemon Chile Oil over the top. Serve immediately, garnished with the coriander (if using).

Shrimp, Pine Nuts, Pesto, & Parmesan

~~~

GARLIC-FLAVORED SHRIMP ARE AN EXTREMELY POPULAR DISH.
ENHANCED WITH BASIL AND PARMESAN CHEESE, THEY MAKE A
WONDERFUL BLEND FOR THIS PIZZA TOPPING.

2 (8-ounce) dough balls (see page 8)
⅔ cup Pizza Sauce (see page 10)
1¼ cups grated mozzarella cheese
7 ounces medium shrimp, peeled and
  deveined
¼ cup Pesto Sauce (see page 11)
½ cup Parmesan cheese shavings
1 red onion, thinly sliced into rings
3 tablespoons pine nuts
small handful of basil, freshly chopped

MAKES 2 MEDIUM PIZZAS

Place two pizza stones or tiles in the oven. Heat the oven to 500°F. Roll out the pizza dough, as described on page 10, so that you have two bases. Cover the bases with the Pizza Sauce and mozzarella cheese, keeping a 1¼-inch border around the edge of the dough clean.

Place the shrimp around the edge of each base in a clock-style pattern. Dollop the Pesto Sauce on each pizza in small spoonfuls. Add the Parmesan cheese and onion rings. Sprinkle the pine nuts and basil over the top.

Using a wide spatula or pizza paddle, gently slide each pizza onto a stone or tile. Cook for 10 minutes. Remove the pizzas from the oven when cooked and golden. Slice each pizza into eight pieces and serve immediately.

Oyster Kilpatrick

~~~

STRICTLY FOR THE OYSTER FANATICS AMONG US, THIS RECIPE
TAKES THE CLASSIC ELEMENTS OF OYSTERS KILPATRICK
AND TURNS THEM INTO A FABULOUS PIZZA.

2 (8-ounce) dough balls (see page 8)
⅔ cup Pizza Sauce (see page 10)
1¼ cups grated mozzarella cheese
10–16 oysters, fresh from their shells
5 ounces bacon slices, without rind,
  cooked and diced
½ small red onion, thinly sliced into rings
1½ ounces Brie cheese, cut into strips
  ¼ inch thick
2 teaspoons freshly chopped dill
¼ cup Worcestershire sauce, or to taste

MAKES 2 MEDIUM PIZZAS

Place two pizza stones or tiles in the oven.
Heat the oven to 500°F. Roll out the pizza
dough, as described on page 10, so that
you have two bases. Cover the bases with
the Pizza Sauce and mozzarella cheese,
keeping a 1¼-inch border around the edge
of the dough clean.

Place the oysters around the edge of each
base in a clock-style pattern. Sprinkle the
bacon over the top of the pizzas. Add the
onion rings. Break the strips of Brie cheese
into chunks and place on top of the onion.
Sprinkle the dill over the top.

Using a wide spatula or pizza paddle,
gently slide each pizza onto a stone or tile.
Cook for 10 minutes. Remove the pizzas
from the oven when cooked and golden.
Slice each pizza into eight pieces and liberally sprinkle the Worcestershire sauce over
the top. Serve immediately.

Wok Lobster

~~~

A JAPANESE-INSPIRED COMBINATION OF LOBSTER WITH BLACK BEANS,
PICKLED GINGER, SCALLIONS, CARROT, AND CRISPY-FRIED LEEK.
THE PICKLED GINGER IS BEST PREPARED A DAY IN ADVANCE. ONCE MADE,
IT WILL LAST INDEFINITELY IF STORED IN AN AIRTIGHT CONTAINER IN
THE REFRIGERATOR. PICKLED GINGER IS A WONDERFUL CONDIMENT
THAT COMPLEMENTS ANY TYPE OF SEAFOOD.

PICKLED GINGER

8 ounces ginger, peeled and cut into paper-
  thin slices
1⅔ cups rice vinegar
¼ cup cider vinegar
4 teaspoons white vinegar
5 teaspoons granulated sugar
5 teaspoons salt

PIZZA

8 ounces lobster meat, broken into large
  chunks
¼ cup black bean sauce (available from
  good supermarkets or Asian food stores)
freshly ground black pepper, to taste
a little peanut oil
a little sesame oil
2 (8-ounce) dough balls (see page 8)
⅔ cup Pizza Sauce (see page 10)
1¼ cups grated mozzarella cheese
1 small carrot, cut into fine julienne
6 scallions, sliced on the angle, Chinese
  style
2 teaspoons pickled ginger

1 leek, white part only, cut into 2-inch
  lengths and thinly sliced into strips
vegetable oil, for deep-frying
salt, to taste
freshly ground black pepper, to taste

MAKES 2 MEDIUM PIZZAS

PICKLED GINGER

Place the ginger in a heatproof bowl and
cover with boiling water. Let stand for 2 minutes. Drain. Transfer the ginger to a large
sterilized jar.

Combine the remaining ingredients in a
saucepan. Stir over a moderate heat until the
sugar and salt dissolve. Pour over the ginger
in the jar and seal. Leave for at least 2–3
hours before using.

Marinate the lobster in the black bean sauce.
Season with black pepper. Heat a wok or
medium frying pan over a moderate heat.

Add some peanut oil and a little sesame oil to the wok or pan. When the oil starts to smoke, add the lobster meat. Turn to sear on all sides and then remove from the wok or pan.

Place two pizza stones or tiles in the oven. Heat the oven to 500°F. Roll out the pizza dough, as described on page 10, so that you have two bases.

Cover the bases with the Pizza Sauce and mozzarella cheese, keeping a 1¼-inch border around the edge of the dough clean. Place the lobster on each base in a clock-style pattern. Add the carrot, scallions, and pickled ginger.

Deep-fry the leek in vegetable oil until lightly golden and crisp. (If you do not have a deep-fryer, half-fill a saucepan with vegetable or peanut oil, heat gently, and cook the leek.) Season with a little salt. Set aside.

Using a wide spatula or pizza paddle, gently slide each pizza onto a stone or tile. Cook for 10 minutes. Remove the pizzas from the oven when cooked and golden. Slice each pizza into eight pieces and serve immediately, garnished with the crispy-fried leek and seasoned with the black pepper.

Scallops, Asparagus, Crème Fraîche, & Almonds

~~~

CRÈME FRAÎCHE IS USED AS THE BASE SAUCE FOR THIS PIZZA. IT RETAINS
ITS SUBTLETY AND BLENDS FANTASTICALLY WITH THE OTHER INGREDIENTS.
BE SURE TO BUY THE FRESHEST SCALLOPS AVAILABLE.

2 teaspoons butter
½ cup sliced almonds
3 tablespoons chopped parsley
grated peel and juice of ½ lemon
¾ cup crème fraîche
2 (8-ounce) dough balls (see page 8)
1¼ cups grated mozzarella cheese
13 ounces scallops, seared in a hot frying
　　pan or skillet until slightly undercooked
　　(see page 6)
2 bunches of asparagus, stems peeled and
　　spears blanched
extra sliced almonds

MAKES 2 MEDIUM PIZZAS

Melt the butter in a frying pan or skillet over a medium heat. Add the almonds and sauté until they just start to color. Add the parsley and sauté for a further minute. Add the lemon zest and then the lemon juice. Remove the pan from the heat. Allow to cool and then combine thoroughly with the crème fraîche.

Place two pizza stones or tiles in the oven. Heat the oven to 500°F. Roll out the pizza dough, as described on page 10, so that you have two bases. Cover the bases with the crème fraîche mixture and then the mozzarella cheese, keeping a 1¼-inch border around the edge of the dough clean.

Place the scallops on the bases in a random pattern. Cut the asparagus spears in half lengthways and chop into 1½-inch lengths. Place on the pizzas. Add a few more sliced almonds.

Using a wide spatula or pizza paddle, gently slide each pizza onto a stone or tile. Cook for 10 minutes. Remove the pizzas from the oven when cooked and golden. Slice each pizza into eight pieces and serve immediately.

Smoked Salmon with Avocado & Brie

~~~

SIMPLE, CLASSIC INGREDIENTS COMBINE TO MAKE THIS
AN IDEAL BRUNCH PIZZA. SERVE WITH A LITTLE OLIVE OIL DRIZZLED
AROUND THE CRUST FOR A MORE FLAVORFUL RESULT.

2 (8-ounce) dough balls (see page 8)
⅔ cup Pizza Sauce (see page 10)
1¼ cups grated mozzarella cheese
5 ounces sliced smoked salmon, broken
   into pieces about 1¼ inches square
1 medium avocado, peeled and quartered,
   then sliced into crescents
½ small red onion, sliced
2 ounces Brie cheese, cut into strips about
   ¼ inch wide
2 teaspoons freshly chopped dill
sour cream, to garnish
freshly ground black pepper, to taste

MAKES 2 MEDIUM PIZZAS

Place two pizza stones or tiles in the oven. Heat the oven to 500°F. Roll out the pizza dough, as described on page 10, so that you have two bases. Cover the bases with the Pizza Sauce and mozzarella cheese, keeping a 1¼-inch border around the edge of the dough clean.

Place the salmon on the bases in a random pattern. Add the avocado and onion. Break the strips of Brie cheese into chunks and place on top of the onion. Sprinkle the dill over the top.

Using a wide spatula or pizza paddle, gently slide each pizza onto a stone or tile. Cook for 10 minutes. Remove the pizzas from the oven when cooked and golden. Slice each pizza into eight pieces and serve immediately, garnished with the sour cream and seasoned with the black pepper.

Barbecued Shrimp with Brie & Coriander

THE BARBECUE IS AS MUCH A PART OF THE IMAGE OF AUSTRALIAN LIFE AS THE BEACH, SO BARBECUE SAUCE SEEMED A LOGICAL PARTNER FOR SHRIMP ON THE TOPPING OF THIS PIZZA.

2 (8-ounce) dough balls (see page 8)
scant ½ cup Pizza Sauce (see page 10)
¼ cup Barbecue Sauce (see page 11)
1¼ cups grated mozzarella cheese
20–24 medium shrimp, cooked, peeled, and deveined
4 ounces bacon slices, without rind, cooked and diced
1 medium red onion, cut into wedges and roasted (see page 12)
2 ounces Brie cheese, cut into strips ¼ inch thick
½ bunch of coriander (cilantro) leaves, chopped
freshly ground black pepper, to taste

MAKES 2 MEDIUM PIZZAS

Place two pizza stones or tiles in the oven. Heat the oven to 500°F. Roll out the pizza dough, as described on page 10, so that you have two bases. Combine the Pizza Sauce and Barbecue Sauce. Cover the bases with this mixture and then sprinkle over the mozzarella cheese, keeping a 1¼-inch border around the edge of the dough clean.

Place the shrimp on each base in a clock-style pattern, with two shrimp in the center. Add the bacon and roast onion. Break the strips of Brie cheese into chunks and place on top of the onion. Sprinkle the coriander over the top.

Using a wide spatula or pizza paddle, gently slide each pizza onto a stone or tile. Cook for 10 minutes. Remove the pizzas from the oven when cooked and golden. Slice each pizza into eight pieces and season with the black pepper. Serve immediately.

Superior Seafood

~~~

A HARVEST OF SEAFOOD WITH DIFFERENT SHAPES GIVES AN INTERESTING
VISUAL APPEAL TO THIS PIZZA. TOP IT OFF BY LEAVING TWO OYSTERS IN THE
SHELL AND PLACING THEM ON EACH PIZZA AS AN UNUSUAL GARNISH.

2 (8-ounce) dough balls (see page 8)
⅔ cup Pizza Sauce (see page 10)
1¼ cups grated mozzarella cheese
4 fresh oysters (plus 2 oysters on the shell
   for garnish (optional))
1 ounce sliced smoked salmon, broken up
   into pieces
3 ounces scallops, cooked (see page 6)
3 ounces shrimp, cooked, peeled, and
   deveined
2 ounces mussels, cooked and shell
   removed (see page 6)
½ small red onion, cut into wedges and
   roasted (see page 12)
⅓ cup Parmesan cheese shavings
2 teaspoons freshly chopped dill
freshly ground black pepper, to taste

MAKES 2 MEDIUM PIZZAS

Place two pizza stones or tiles in the oven. Heat the oven to 500°F. Roll out the pizza dough, as described on page 10, so that you have two bases. Cover the bases with the Pizza Sauce and mozzarella cheese, keeping a 1¼-inch border around the edge of the dough clean.

Divide the seafood evenly between the two pizzas. Place on the bases in a random pattern, ensuring that the pieces are not piled on top of each other. Add the onion and Parmesan cheese. Sprinkle the dill over the top.

Using a wide spatula or pizza paddle, gently slide each pizza onto a stone or tile. Cook for 10 minutes. Remove the pizzas from the oven when cooked and golden. Slice each pizza into eight pieces and serve immediately, seasoned with the black pepper.

Grilled Tuna with Orange Chile Oil

~~~

AN INFUSION OF CHILE AND ORANGE IS DRIZZLED OVER THE CHARRED
TUNA ON THIS PIZZA FOR AN UNBEATABLE TASTE. FOR A MORE SPECTACULAR
PRESENTATION, GARNISH WITH SOME CRISPY-FRIED RICE NOODLES.

ORANGE CHILE OIL

scant ½ cup peanut oil
2 teaspoons sesame oil
4 teaspoons red chile powder
½ teaspoon black peppercorns
½ teaspoon crushed garlic
1½ teaspoons chopped fresh ginger
½ teaspoon chopped dried lemon grass
grated peel of 1 orange

PIZZA

a little olive oil
7 ounces tuna steaks
2 (8-ounce) dough balls (see page 8)
⅔ cup Pizza Sauce (see page 10)
1¼ cups grated mozzarella cheese
2 red bell peppers, roasted, peeled, and
  cut into chunks (see page 12)
4 scallions, sliced on the angle, Chinese
  style
¼ cup Orange Chile Oil
rice noodles, crispy-fried, to garnish
  (optional)

MAKES 2 MEDIUM PIZZAS

ORANGE CHILE OIL

Combine the peanut and sesame oils in a
saucepan. Place over a gentle heat until the
oil mixture starts to shimmer. Be extremely
careful as the oil may splutter.

Place the chile powder, black peppercorns, garlic, ginger, and lemon grass in
a stainless steel bowl. Carefully pour the
shimmering oil over the top and let stand for
3 minutes.

Add the orange peel and let the oil stand
for at least 24 hours before using. This oil
will keep indefinitely if stored in an airtight
jar or bottle in a cool, dark place.

Heat a little olive oil in a frying pan or skillet
until very hot. Sear the tuna steaks on one
side only. Alternatively, sear the tuna on the
grill bars of a barbecue or broiler. Allow the
tuna to cool completely before cutting into
large pieces.

Place two pizza stones or tiles in the oven. Heat the oven to 500°F. Roll out the pizza dough, as described on page 10, so that you have two bases. Cover the bases with the Pizza Sauce and mozzarella cheese, keeping a 1¼-inch border around the edge of the dough clean.

Place the tuna on the bases in a clock-style pattern, placing any leftover tuna in a similar pattern in the center of each pizza. Be careful not to overload the pizzas with tuna. Add the bell peppers and scallions.

Using a wide spatula or pizza paddle, gently slide each pizza onto a stone or tile. Cook for 10 minutes.

Remove the pizzas from the oven when cooked and golden. Slice each pizza into eight pieces. Heap a pile of rice noodles in the center of each pizza (if using). Drizzle a little Orange Chile Oil over the top and serve immediately.

The Ultimate

~~~

THIS IS A VERY SPECIAL PIZZA MADE WITH PREMIUM SMOKED SALMON
AND TOPPED WITH SALMON ROE AND CRÈME FRAÎCHE. PLACE THE
SALMON ON THE PIZZA PARTWAY THROUGH COOKING SO THAT IT IS
ONLY SLIGHTLY WARMED AND RETAINS ITS DELICATE FLAVOR.

2 (8-ounce) dough balls (see page 8)

⅔ cup Pizza Sauce (see page 10)

1¼ cups grated mozzarella cheese

1 red onion, thinly sliced into rings

4 teaspoons small capers, rinsed of any salt or brine

½ bunch of dill, freshly chopped

7 ounces sliced smoked salmon

a little extra virgin olive oil

scant 1 cup crème fraîche

2 ounces salmon roe caviar or sevruga caviar

2 dill sprigs, to garnish

freshly ground black pepper, to taste

MAKES 2 MEDIUM PIZZAS

Place two pizza stones or tiles in the oven. Heat the oven to 500°F. Roll out the pizza dough, as described on page 10, so that you have two bases. Cover the bases with the Pizza Sauce and mozzarella cheese, keeping a 1¼-inch border around the edge of the dough clean.

Place the onion on the bases in a random pattern, reserving some for later use. Add some capers. Sprinkle the dill over the top.

Using a wide spatula or pizza paddle, gently slide each pizza onto a stone or tile. Cook for 7 minutes. Remove the pizzas from the oven and lay the salmon out over each base so that as much surface area as possible is covered. Place a few more onion rings on top of the salmon. Return to the oven and cook for a further 3–4 minutes.

Remove the pizzas from the oven and drizzle generously with the extra virgin olive oil. Slice each pizza into eight pieces. Place a large dollop of crème fraîche in the center of each pizza. Dollop a large spoonful of salmon roe beside the crème fraîche. Serve immediately, garnished with the dill sprigs and seasoned with black pepper.

A Vegetarian
HARVEST

THERE REALLY ISN'T ANY VEGETABLE THAT CANNOT BE
USED IN CREATING GOURMET PIZZAS. IT IS SIMPLY A
MATTER OF WORKING OUT THE BEST WAY TO CUT AND
PREPARE THE VEGETABLE, AND OF JUDGING HOW WELL
COOKED IT SHOULD BE WHEN THE PIZZA IS REMOVED
FROM THE OVEN. AS WITH ANY INGREDIENTS USED FOR
TOPPINGS, FRESHNESS AND THE SELECTION OF
GRADE-A PRODUCE ARE OF PRIME IMPORTANCE.

ALSO, THE DIFFERENCE BETWEEN USING FRESHLY
CHOPPED HERBS AND THEIR DRIED EQUIVALENT IS
ENORMOUS. ALWAYS TRY TO USE FRESH HERBS
WHERE INDICATED. THE FRAGRANCE RELEASED
FROM THE FRESH HERB IS UNOBTAINABLE
ELSEWHERE. FRESH IS DEFINITELY BEST.

Cherry Tomato, Ricotta, Roast Garlic, & Pesto

~~~

SIMPLE INGREDIENTS KEEP THE FLAVORS OF THIS PIZZA BASIC, BUT STILL
TASTY. IF YOU'RE NOT KEEN ON GARLIC, OMIT IT AND ADD EXTRA FRESH BASIL.

2 (8-ounce) dough balls (see page 8)
scant 1 cup Pesto Sauce (see page 11)
½ pint cherry tomatoes, halved
3 ounces ricotta cheese
4 teaspoons roast garlic purée (see page 13)
½ bunch of basil, freshly chopped

MAKES 2 MEDIUM PIZZAS

Place two pizza stones or tiles in the oven. Heat the oven to 500°F. Roll out the pizza dough, as described on page 10, so that you have two bases. Cover the bases with the Pesto Sauce and mozzarella cheese, keeping a 1¼-inch border around the edge of the dough clean.

Place the cherry tomatoes on the bases in a random pattern, leaving spaces for other ingredients to fall into. Dot the pizzas with small teaspoons of ricotta. Add the roast garlic in dollops. Sprinkle the basil over the top.

Using a wide spatula or pizza paddle, gently slide each pizza onto a stone or tile. Cook for 10 minutes. Remove the pizzas from the oven when cooked and golden. Slice each pizza into eight pieces and serve immediately.

Smoked Chile, Parmesan Cheese, & Roma Tomatoes

THIS TOPPING TAKES THE AGE-OLD FAITHFUL OF CHEESE AND TOMATO
TO A NEW EXTREME WITH THE INTRODUCTION OF CHIPOTLE CHILE PEPPERS—
A FIERY REBIRTH OF AN OLD CLASSIC.

2 (8-ounce) dough balls (see page 8)

scant 1 cup crème fraîche

1¼ cups grated mozzarella cheese

4 Roma (plum) tomatoes, sliced into
rounds

¾ cup Parmesan cheese shavings

4 smoked chipotle chile peppers, seeded
and finely chopped (jalapeño or fresh
Thai red chile peppers may be
substituted)

MAKES 2 MEDIUM PIZZAS

Place two pizza stones or tiles in the oven. Heat the oven to 500°F. Roll out the pizza dough, as described on page 10, so that you have two bases. Cover the bases with the crème fraîche and mozzarella cheese, keeping a 1¼-inch border around the edge of the dough clean.

Place the tomato slices on the bases in a random pattern. Add the Parmesan cheese. Sprinkle the chile peppers over the top.

Using a wide spatula or pizza paddle, gently slide each pizza onto a stone or tile. Cook for 10 minutes. Remove the pizzas from the oven when cooked and golden. Slice each pizza into eight pieces and serve immediately.

Goat Cheese, Broccoli, Pine Nuts, & Basil

~~~

THE GOAT CHEESE PROVIDES A GOOD CONTRAST TO THE BROCCOLI ON THIS TOPPING, AND A CREAMY BACKGROUND FLAVOR. IF DESIRED, YOU COULD EASILY ADD SMOKED HAM OR PROSCIUTTO TO THIS PIZZA.

2 (8-ounce) dough balls (see page 8)
⅔ cup Pizza Sauce (see page 10)
1¼ cups grated mozzarella cheese
2–3 heads broccoli, cut into florets and blanched
4 ounces goat cheese, cut into chunks
1 red onion, thinly sliced into rings
4 teaspoons pine nuts
½ bunch of basil, freshly chopped

MAKES 2 MEDIUM PIZZAS

Place two pizza stones or tiles in the oven. Heat the oven to 500°F. Roll out the pizza dough, as described on page 10, so that you have two bases. Cover the bases with the Pizza Sauce and mozzarella cheese, keeping a 1¼-inch border around the edge of the dough clean.

Place the broccoli on the bases in a random pattern. Add the goat cheese and lay the onion rings over the top. Sprinkle with the pine nuts and top with the basil.

Using a wide spatula or pizza paddle, gently slide each pizza onto a stone or tile. Cook for 10 minutes. Remove the pizzas from the oven when cooked and golden. Slice each pizza into eight pieces and serve immediately.

Napoli

~~~~~

THE RECIPE IS BASED ON THE TRADITIONAL NAPOLI TOPPING,
BUT WITH THE ADDED REFINEMENT OF ROAST GARLIC AND FRESH ROSEMARY.
THE PERFECT PIZZA TO KEEP THE VAMPIRES AWAY . . . AND ANYONE ELSE!

2 (8-ounce) dough balls (see page 8)
⅔ cup Pizza Sauce (see page 10)
2 cups mozzarella cheese
13 ounces tomatoes, roasted and cut into
   quarters lengthwise if necessary
   (see page 12)
2 tablespoons roast garlic purée
   (see page 13)
½ bunch of fresh rosemary, stems
   discarded and leaves chopped
freshly ground black pepper, to taste

MAKES 2 MEDIUM PIZZAS

Place two pizza stones or tiles in the oven. Heat the oven to 500°F. Roll out the pizza dough, as described on page 10, so that you have two bases. Cover the bases with the Pizza Sauce and 1¼ cups of the mozzarella cheese, keeping a 1¼-inch border around the edge of the dough clean. Reserve the remaining cheese.

Place the roast tomato on the bases in a clock-style pattern, placing a couple of pieces in the center of each base. Top with the extra mozzarella cheese. Add the roast garlic (if you want a really good garlic "fix" then use as much as you like). Sprinkle the rosemary over the top.

Using a wide spatula or pizza paddle, gently slide each pizza onto a stone or tile. Cook for 10 minutes. Remove the pizzas from the oven when cooked and golden. Slice each pizza into eight pieces and serve immediately, seasoned with the black pepper.

Cheeseaholic

~~~

FOR THOSE AMONG US WHO ABSOLUTELY ADORE CHEESE. THE FIVE CHEESES
USED GIVE THIS PIZZA A SHARP YET CREAMY TEXTURE. SPINACH BALANCES THE
OVERPOWERING NATURE OF THE CHEESE, GIVING A MORE ROUNDED FLAVOR.

SPINACH PURÉE
a little oil
½ yellow onion, diced
scant ½ cup whipping cream
pinch of nutmeg
½ bunch of spinach, rinsed and stems
   discarded

PIZZA
2 (8-ounce) dough balls (see page 8)
⅔ cup Pizza Sauce (see page 10)
1¼ cups grated mozzarella cheese
2 ounces goat cheese, broken into pieces
2 ounces blue cheese, broken into pieces
2 ounces Brie cheese, cut into slices
   ¼ inch thick
2–3 tablespoons chopped walnuts
   (optional)
½ cup Parmesan cheese shavings
a few spinach leaves (optional)
chives, finely chopped, to garnish

MAKES 2 MEDIUM PIZZAS

SPINACH PURÉE
Heat a little oil in a small saucepan. Add the
onion and sauté until transparent. Add the
cream and nutmeg. Bring to the boil and
add the spinach. Mix thoroughly and remove
from the heat. Place the spinach mixture in
an electric blender or food processor. Blend
into a smooth purée and allow to cool
before using.

Place two pizza stones or tiles in the oven.
Heat the oven to 500°F. Roll out the pizza
dough, as described on page 10, so that
you have two bases. Cover the bases with
the Pizza Sauce and mozzarella cheese,
keeping a 1¼-inch border around the edge
of the dough clean.
   Place small spoonfuls of the spinach
purée all over the bases. Add the goat,
blue, and Brie cheeses in a random pattern.
Sprinkle with the walnuts (if using). Add the
Parmesan cheese. Garnish with the spinach
leaves (if using).
   Using a wide spatula or pizza paddle,
gently slide each pizza onto a stone or tile.
Cook for 10 minutes. Remove from the oven
when cooked and golden. Slice each pizza
into eight pieces. Serve immediately, garnished with the chives.

Olive

~~~

THIS PIZZA IS FOR THE OLIVE LOVERS AMONG US. SEEK OUT THE
BEST-QUALITY MARINATED, UNPITTED OLIVES FROM YOUR LOCAL
SUPERMARKET FOR THIS RECIPE. THEY HAVE MORE FLAVOR THAN
THE BOTTLED, COMMERCIALLY CORED VARIETIES.

2 (8-ounce) dough balls (see page 8)
⅔ cup Pizza Sauce(see page 10)
1¾ cups grated mozzarella cheese
¼ cup olive purée (available from good
   supermarkets)
5 ounces tomatoes, roasted (see page 12)
1 red onion, cut into wedges and roasted
   (see page 12)
⅓ cup kalamata olives, pitted and cut into
   quarters
⅓ cup green olives, pitted and cut into
   quarters

MAKES 2 MEDIUM PIZZAS

Place two pizza stones or tiles in the oven.
Heat the oven to 500°F. Roll out the pizza
dough, as described on page 10, so that
you have two bases. Cover the bases with
the Pizza Sauce and 1¼ cups of the mozzarella cheese, keeping a 1¼-inch border
around the edge of the dough clean. Reserve
the remaining cheese.

Dot the olive purée in small portions
(about ½ teaspoon) all over the bases. Add
the roast tomato and roast onion. Scatter the
kalamata and green olives over the top. Top
with the extra mozzarella cheese.

Using a wide spatula or pizza paddle,
gently slide each pizza onto a stone or tile.
Cook for 10 minutes. Remove the pizzas
from the oven when cooked and golden.
Slice each pizza into eight pieces and serve
immediately.

Pesto

~~~~~

THIS TOPPING IS SIMPLICITY IN ITSELF—"THE" CLASSIC PIZZA. BASIL,
GARLIC, PINE NUTS, AND RED ONION ARE BLENDED TOGETHER AND
SMOTHERED OVER THE BASE, AND THEN TOPPED WITH EXTRA CHEESE.

2 (8-ounce) dough balls (see page 8)
scant 1 cup Pesto Sauce (see page 11)
1¼ cups grated mozzarella cheese
¾ cup Parmesan cheese shavings
1 large red onion, thinly sliced into rings
4 teaspoons pine nuts
½ bunch of basil, freshly chopped
freshly ground black pepper, to taste

MAKES 2 MEDIUM PIZZAS

Place two pizza stones or tiles in the oven. Heat the oven to 500°F. Roll out the pizza dough, as described on page 10, so that you have two bases. Cover the bases with the Pesto Sauce and mozzarella cheese, keeping a 1¼-inch border around the edge of the dough clean.

Lay the Parmesan cheese on the bases. Top with plenty of onion rings. Sprinkle with the pine nuts and basil.

Using a wide spatula or pizza paddle, gently slide each pizza onto a stone or tile. Cook for 10 minutes. Remove the pizzas from the oven when cooked and golden. Slice each pizza into eight pieces and serve immediately, seasoned with the black pepper.

Tomato, Goat Cheese, & Olives with Pesto

~~~

THE SIMPLE, ROBUST FLAVORS OF TOMATO, GOAT CHEESE, AND OLIVES CHARACTERIZE THIS PIZZA.

2 (8-ounce) dough balls (see page 8)

⅔ cup Pizza Sauce (see page 10)

2 Roma (plum) tomatoes, sliced into rounds

scant ½ cup Pesto Sauce (see page 11)

2 tablespoons kalamata olives, pitted and cut into quarters

4 ounces goat cheese, cut into chunks

½ bunch of basil, freshly chopped

freshly ground black pepper, to taste

MAKES 2 MEDIUM PIZZAS

Place two pizza stones or tiles in the oven. Heat the oven to 500°F. Roll out the pizza dough, as described on page 10, so that you have two bases. Cover the bases with the Pizza Sauce and mozzarella cheese, keeping a 1¼-inch border around the edge of the dough clean.

Place the tomato slices on the bases in a clock-style pattern, placing two pieces in the center of each base. Using a teaspoon, place small amounts of the Pesto Sauce in between the tomato slices. Add the olives and goat cheese. Sprinkle the basil generously over the top.

Using a wide spatula or pizza paddle, gently slide each pizza onto a stone or tile. Cook for 10 minutes. Remove the pizzas from the oven when cooked and golden. Slice each pizza into eight pieces and serve immediately, seasoned with the black pepper.

Triple Tomato with Lemon Thyme

~~~

THIS IS ESSENTIALLY A "RED" PIZZA. IT HAS THREE DIFFERENT
TYPES OF TOMATO ON ITS TOPPING—SUN-DRIED, ROASTED, AND CHERRY—
ALL TOPPED WITH A TANGY CHEDDAR CHEESE.

2 (8-ounce) dough balls (see page 8)
⅔ cup Pizza Sauce (see page 10)
1¼ cups grated mozzarella cheese
½ cup sun-dried tomatoes (drained of oil), diced
8 ounces tomatoes, roasted (see page 12)
1 red bell pepper, roasted and cut into chunks (see page 12)
½ pint cherry tomatoes, halved
½ cup grated Cheddar cheese
½ bunch of lemon thyme leaves, chopped

MAKES 2 MEDIUM PIZZAS

Place two pizza stones or tiles in the oven. Heat the oven to 500°F. Roll out the pizza dough, as described on page 10, so that you have two bases. Cover the bases with the Pizza Sauce and mozzarella cheese, keeping a 1¼-inch border around the edge of the dough clean.

Arrange the sun-dried tomato on the bases first. Place the roast tomatoes on the bases in a clock-style pattern, placing two tomatoes in the middle of each base. Add the red bell pepper and cherry tomato. Top with the Cheddar cheese. Sprinkle the lemon thyme over the top.

Using a wide spatula or pizza paddle, gently slide each pizza onto a stone or tile. Cook for 10 minutes. Remove the pizzas from the oven when cooked and golden. Slice each pizza into eight pieces and serve immediately.

Spinach, Broccoli, & Chile Cream Cheese

~~~

THE UNIQUE BASE SAUCE OF CHILE CREAM CHEESE MAKES THIS PIZZA
ESPECIALLY DELICIOUS. THE OTHER TOPPING INGREDIENTS SINK INTO THE
CREAM CHEESE AND PERMEATE IT WITH EVEN MORE FLAVOR.

CHILE CREAM CHEESE
5 ounces cream cheese
juice of 1 lemon
1 teaspoon chile paste

PIZZA
2 (8-ounce) dough balls (see page 8)
1¼ cups grated mozzarella cheese
2 heads of broccoli, cut into florets and
　blanched
1 red bell pepper, diced
12 button mushrooms, sliced
1 red onion, thinly sliced into rings
extra mozzarella cheese, grated (optional)
16 baby spinach leaves, rubbed with a
　little olive oil

MAKES 2 MEDIUM PIZZAS

CHILE CREAM CHEESE
Thoroughly combine the cream cheese,
lemon juice, and chile paste. This mixture
forms the base sauce for this pizza.

Place two pizza stones or tiles in the oven.
Heat the oven to 500°F. Roll out the pizza
dough, as described on page 10, so that
you have two bases. Cover the bases with
the Chile Cream Cheese and mozzarella
cheese, keeping a 1¼-inch border around
the edge of the dough clean.

Place the broccoli on the bases in a
random pattern, leaving spaces for other
ingredients to fall into. Add the red bell pepper, mushrooms, and onion. Sprinkle a little
extra mozzarella cheese over the top (if
using). Add the spinach leaves.

Using a wide spatula or pizza paddle,
gently slide each pizza onto a stone or tile.
Cook for 10 minutes. Remove the pizzas
from the oven when cooked and golden.
Slice each pizza into eight pieces and
serve immediately.

Roast Vegetables with Goat Cheese & Basil

〜〜〜

OUR ORIGINAL VEGETARIAN PIZZA, WHICH STARTED LIFE AS LEFTOVERS FROM A
ROAST DINNER. ONE DAY I USED LEFTOVER ROAST VEGETABLES ON A PIZZA BASE
AT HOME—A SPONTANEOUS IDEA THAT'S BECOME A FIRM FAVORITE.

1 large eggplant, cut into slices ¼ inch thick
1 medium sweet potato, cut into slices
   ¼ inch thick
a little oil
salt and freshly ground black pepper,
   to taste
2 (8-ounce) dough balls (see page 8)
⅔ cup Pizza Sauce (see page 10)
1¼ cups grated mozzarella cheese
½ cup sun-dried tomatoes (drained of oil),
   diced
3 tablespoons roast garlic purée
   (see page 13)
2 ounces goat cheese, cut into chunks
½ bunch of basil leaves, chopped

MAKES 2 MEDIUM PIZZAS

Preheat the oven to 325°. Place the eggplant and sweet potato on a lightly oiled tray. Season with salt and pepper. Cover the tray with baking parchment. Roast in the oven for 12–15 minutes, or until cooked. Allow to cool. Cut the slices into quarters.

Place two pizza stones or tiles in the oven. Heat the oven to 500°F. Roll out the pizza dough, as described on page 10, so that you have two bases. Cover the bases with the Pizza Sauce and mozzarella cheese, keeping a 1¼-inch border around the edge of the dough clean.

Place the sun-dried tomatoes on the bases. Place the eggplant and sweet potato on the bases in a random pattern. Dot the roast garlic on in very small spoonfuls. Add the goat cheese. Sprinkle the basil over the top.

Using a wide spatula or pizza paddle, gently slide each pizza onto a stone or tile. Cook for 10 minutes. Remove the pizzas from the oven when cooked and golden. Slice each pizza into eight pieces and serve immediately.

Vegetarian

~~~

A VARIATION OF ITS PREDECESSOR, ROAST VEGETABLES WITH GOAT CHEESE AND BASIL, BUT WITHOUT THE GARLIC. AN EQUALLY TASTY PIZZA NONETHELESS.

1 large eggplant, cut into slices ¼ inch thick

1 medium sweet potato, cut into slices ¼ inch thick

a little oil

salt and freshly ground black pepper, to taste

2 (8-ounce) dough balls (see page 8)

⅔ cup Pizza Sauce (see page 10)

1¼ cups grated mozzarella cheese

1 red onion, cut into wedges and roasted (see page 12)

½ pint cherry tomatoes, halved

2½ ounces goat cheese, cut into chunks

½ bunch of basil leaves, chopped

freshly ground black pepper, to taste

MAKES 2 MEDIUM PIZZAS

Preheat the oven to 325°. Place the eggplant and sweet potato on a lightly oiled tray. Season with salt and pepper. Cover the tray with baking parchment. Roast in the oven for 12–15 minutes, or until cooked. Allow to cool and cut the slices into quarters.

Place two pizza stones or tiles in the oven. Heat the oven to 500°F. Roll out the pizza dough, as described on page 10, so that you have two bases. Cover the bases with the Pizza Sauce and mozzarella cheese, keeping a 1¼-inch border around the edge of the dough clean.

When topping this pizza, be careful not to stack one ingredient on top of the other. Place the sweet potato on the bases in a random pattern. Add the eggplant, onion, cherry tomatoes, and goat cheese. Sprinkle the basil over the top.

Using a wide spatula or pizza paddle, gently slide each pizza onto a stone or tile. Cook for 10 minutes. Remove the pizzas from the oven when cooked and golden. Slice each pizza into eight pieces and serve immediately, seasoned with the black pepper.

Vegetarian Supreme

〜〜〜

THIS PIZZA IS MORE MEDITERRANEAN IN FLAVOR THAN THE VEGETARIAN,
WITH ARTICHOKES REPLACING THE SWEET POTATO. SUN-DRIED TOMATOES
AND FETA CHEESE COULD EASILY BE ADDED TO MAKE THIS EVEN MORE
OF A VEGETARIAN EXTRAVAGANZA.

2 (8-ounce) dough balls (see page 8)
⅔ cup Pizza Sauce (see page 10)
1¼ cups grated mozzarella cheese
5 ounces tomatoes, roasted (see page 12)
1 red bell pepper, roasted and cut into
chunks (see page 12)
2 globe artichokes, halved then cut into
quarters
6 button mushrooms, sliced and rubbed
with a little olive oil
2 tablespoons black olives, pitted and cut
into quarters
4 teaspoons roast garlic purée (see page 13)
1 red onion, thinly sliced into rings
extra mozzarella cheese, grated (optional)

MAKES 2 MEDIUM PIZZAS

Place two pizza stones or tiles in the oven. Heat the oven to 500°F. Roll out the pizza dough, as described on page 10, so that you have two bases. Cover the bases with the Pizza Sauce and mozzarella cheese, keeping a 1¼-inch border around the edge of the dough clean.

Place the roast tomatoes on the bases in a random pattern. Add the roast red bell pepper, artichokes, mushrooms, olives, and garlic. Lay the onion rings over the top. Sprinkle the extra mozzarella cheese (if using) over the top to hold the ingredients in place.

Using a wide spatula or pizza paddle, gently slide each pizza onto a stone or tile. Cook for 10 minutes. Remove the pizzas from the oven when cooked and golden. Slice each pizza into eight pieces and serve immediately.

Margherita

~~~

THIS PIZZA IS PROBABLY THE CLOSEST WE MAKE TO A TRADITIONAL TOPPING AT THE RED CENTRE. IT WAS NAMED AFTER THE QUEEN OF ITALY IN THE EIGHTEENTH CENTURY, PROVIDING A SALUTE TO THE COLORS OF THE FLAG.

2 (8-ounce) dough balls (see page 8)
⅔ cup Pizza Sauce (see page 10)
1¼ cups grated mozzarella cheese
10 ounces tomatoes, roasted and cut into quarters lengthwise if necessary (see page 12)
¾ cup Parmesan cheese shavings
1 red onion, thinly sliced into rings
4 teaspoons pine nuts
½ bunch of basil, freshly chopped
freshly ground black pepper, to taste

MAKES 2 MEDIUM PIZZAS

Place two pizza stones or tiles in the oven. Heat the oven to 500°F. Roll out the pizza dough, as described on page 10, so that you have two bases. Cover the bases with the Pizza Sauce and mozzarella cheese, keeping a 1¼-inch border around the edge of the dough clean.

Place the roast tomato on the bases in a clock-style pattern, placing a couple of pieces of tomato in the center of each base. Top with the Parmesan cheese. Add the onion and pine nuts. Sprinkle the basil over the top.

Using a wide spatula or pizza paddle, gently slide each pizza onto a stone or tile. Cook for 10 minutes. Remove the pizzas from the oven when cooked and golden. Slice each pizza into eight pieces and serve immediately, seasoned with the black pepper.

Pear, Gorgonzola, & Pine Nuts

~~~

THIS PIZZA COULD EASILY BE SERVED AS A SUBSTITUTE FOR EITHER A CHEESE
PLATE OR A DESSERT. GORGONZOLA IS A VERY STRONG, CREAMY CHEESE
WHICH MELTS EXTREMELY WELL.

2 (8-ounce) dough balls (see page 8)
⅓ cup Pizza Sauce (see page 10)
¾ cup grated mozzarella cheese
1 large, firm pear (such as Packham),
　peeled, cored, and sliced lengthwise
2 ounces Gorgonzola cheese, cut into
　chunks
3 tablespoons pine nuts or walnuts

MAKES 2 INDIVIDUAL PIZZAS

Place two pizza stones or tiles in the oven. Heat the oven to 500°F. Roll out the pizza dough, as described on page 10, so that you have two bases. Find a plate approximately 7 inches in diameter and place it face down on one of the bases. Take a sharp knife and run it around the outside of the plate to cut a smaller base. Remove the plate. You should now have a round, smooth-edged base. Repeat with the other base.

Cover the bases with the Pizza Sauce and mozzarella cheese, keeping a ½-inch border around the edge of the dough clean. Arrange the sliced pear on the bases in a clock-style pattern, so that the points of the pear meet in the center. Add the Gorgonzola cheese in a random pattern. Sprinkle the pine nuts (or walnuts) over the top.

Using a wide spatula or pizza paddle, gently slide each pizza onto a stone or tile. Cook for 8 minutes. Remove the pizzas from the oven when cooked and golden. Slice each pizza into four pieces and serve immediately.

Deep South

~~~

THIS IS ESSENTIALLY A VEGETARIAN PIZZA, BUT IT ALSO TASTES
DELICIOUS WITH THE ADDITION OF CHICKEN.

2 (8-ounce) dough balls (see page 8)
scant ½ cup Pesto Sauce (see page 11)
1¼ cups grated mozzarella cheese
½ bunch of dill, freshly chopped
2 leeks, white part only, rinsed and sliced
1 cup sun-dried tomatoes (drained of oil), diced
¾ cup roast corn kernels (see page 34–35) (canned corn kernels can be also be used)
1 red bell pepper, diced
salt and freshly ground black pepper, to taste
2 ounces Brie cheese, cut into strips ¼ inch thick

MAKES 2 MEDIUM PIZZAS

Place two pizza stones or tiles in the oven. Heat the oven to 500°F. Roll out the pizza dough, as described on page 10, so that you have two bases. Cover the bases with the Pesto Sauce and mozzarella cheese, keeping a 1¼-inch border around the edge of the dough clean. Sprinkle the dill over the top.

Steam or blanch the leeks until just cooked. Refresh in icy cold water to prevent the leeks from cooking further. Drain and place in a bowl. Add the sun-dried tomatoes, corn kernels, and red bell pepper. Season with salt and pepper. Mix thoroughly. Sprinkle the mixture over the bases. Break the strips of Brie cheese into chunks and place on the bases in a random pattern.

Using a wide spatula or pizza paddle, gently slide each pizza onto a stone or tile. Cook for 10 minutes. Remove the pizzas from the oven when cooked and golden. Slice each pizza into eight pieces and serve immediately.

Beet and Goat Cheese

~~~

THE STRIKING COLOR AND CONTRASTING FLAVORS OF THE TOPPING MAKE
THIS A STUNNING VEGETARIAN PIZZA. COLD CUTS, LEFTOVER ROAST BEEF,
OR PASTRAMI CAN BE ADDED TO COMPLEMENT THE FLAVORS.

BEET RELISH
4 teaspoons olive oil
6–8 baby beets, peeled and grated
½ cup raspberry vinegar
½ cup granulated sugar

PIZZA
2 (8-ounce) dough balls (see page 8)
⅔ cup Pizza Sauce (see page 10)
1¼ cups grated mozzarella cheese
4 ounces goat cheese, cut into chunks
3 Roma (plum) tomatoes, sliced
20 baby beet leaves
½ bunch of chives, freshly chopped

MAKES 2 MEDIUM PIZZAS

BEET RELISH
Put the olive oil and beet in a small sauce-pan. Cook over a gentle heat for 5 minutes. Add the vinegar and sugar. Cover the saucepan with a lid and continue to cook gently for 15 minutes, until the beet becomes soft. Remove from the heat and allow to cool.

Place two pizza stones or tiles in the oven. Heat the oven to 500°F. Roll out the pizza dough, as described on page 10, so that you have two bases.

Cover the bases with the Pizza Sauce and mozzarella cheese, keeping a 1¼-inch border around the edge of the dough clean. Place the goat cheese and tomatoes on the bases in a random pattern.

Using a wide spatula or pizza paddle, gently slide each pizza onto a stone or tile. Cook for 10 minutes. Remove the pizzas from the oven when cooked and golden. Slice each pizza into eight pieces. Distribute the baby beet leaves over each pizza. (If you are using meat on the pizza, place it on now.) Place a large spoonful of Beet Relish in the middle of each pizza. Sprinkle with the chives and serve immediately.

Garden Fresh
SALADS

THE FOLLOWING SALAD CAN BE CONSIDERED
ACCOMPANIMENTS TO ANY OF THE SAVORY PIZZAS IN
THIS BOOK OR, INDEED, ANY MEALS. THEY ARE SIMPLE
TO MAKE AND THE DRESSINGS WILL LAST FOR SOME
TIME IF STORED IN THE REFRIGERATOR.

WHEN RINSING SALAD LEAVES, IT IS IMPORTANT TO BE
GENTLE IN DOING SO. FILL A LARGE BOWL WITH WATER
AND PLACE YOUR LEAVES IN IT. SWIRL THEM GENTLY
TO REMOVE ANY DIRT AND GRIT. IF YOU HAVE A SALAD
SPINNER, USE THIS TO SPIN-DRY THE LEAVES; OTHERWISE,
GIVE THE LEAVES A VIGOROUS SHAKE AND LEAVE THEM
TO DRAIN IN A COLANDER UNTIL NEEDED.

THERE IS NOW AN ALMOST INFINITE RANGE OF GOURMET
SALAD LEAVES AVAILABLE FROM YOUR GREENGROCER OR
SUPERMARKET. THIS MEANS YOU CAN CHOOSE YOUR OWN
"TAILOR-MADE" ASSORTMENT OF MIXED LEAVES OR
MESCLUN. AS WITH ANY VEGETABLES, ALWAYS PICK THE
FRESHEST LEAVES AND HERBS AVAILABLE.

Caesar Salad

~~~

CAESAR SALAD IS A WORLDWIDE FAVORITE, WITH AS MANY VARIATIONS AS COUNTRIES IT IS FOUND IN. HERE'S OUR PARTICULAR VERSION OF THIS CLASSIC.

DRESSING
3 egg yolks
½ teaspoon crushed garlic
2 teaspoons Dijon mustard
3–4 anchovy fillets
2 teaspoons champagne or white wine vinegar
⅔ cup peanut oil
⅓ cup olive oil
salt and ground white pepper, to taste

SALAD
a little olive oil
1 clove garlic, crushed
4 slices stale bread, cut into dice, or ⅓ stale baguette, cut into thin slices
4–5 slices bacon, rind removed
1 head romaine lettuce, cut into strips 1¼ inches wide, rinsed and dried
½ cup Parmesan cheese shavings
freshly ground black pepper, to taste
freshly chopped chives, to garnish

SERVES 4

DRESSING
Place the egg yolks, garlic, Dijon mustard, anchovy fillets, and 1 teaspoon of the vinegar in an electric blender or food processor. Blend or process until the ingredients turn pale and start to thicken slightly. Combine the peanut and olive oils. With the motor running, slowly add the oil to the egg yolk mixture, a few drops at a time at first and then in a steady stream, until all the oil is incorporated. If the dressing is too thick, thin out with the remaining vinegar. If still too thick, add a little hot water. Season with salt and pepper.

The strength of the garlic and anchovies can be varied to suit individual tastes, or even omitted. This dressing will last for up to 2 weeks if stored in an airtight container in the refrigerator.

Preheat the oven to 325°. Combine a little olive oil with the garlic. Place the bread on a baking sheet. Drizzle with the olive oil. Bake until golden and crisp, about 10 minutes. Place the bacon slices on a wire rack with a roasting pan underneath. (As the bacon cooks, the fat will fall into the pan, leaving you with crispy bacon.) Roast in the oven until crisp. Allow to cool and break into pieces.

Place the romaine lettuce in a bowl. Add the Parmesan cheese, croutons, and bacon. Season with the black pepper. Add just enough dressing to coat the leaves. Toss through with a pair of tongs. Serve garnished with the chives.

Marinated & Roast Vegetables with Baby Leaves, Feta, & Olives

A DELICIOUS MIXTURE OF ROASTED AND MARINATED VEGETABLES, DRESSED WITH A SIMPLE BALSAMIC VINEGAR AND EXTRA-VIRGIN OLIVE OIL VINAIGRETTE.

1 medium red onion, cut into wedges

a little olive oil

1 yellow zucchini, cut lengthwise into ½-inch strips

1 green zucchini, cut lengthwise into ½-inch strips

2 ounces mixed baby salad leaves or mesclun, rinsed and dried

1 red bell pepper, roasted, peeled, and cut into strips (see page 12)

6 marinated artichoke halves, cut into pieces

6–8 sun-dried tomatoes, drained of oil and cut into quarters

2 ounces feta cheese, thinly sliced

8–10 kalamata olives, pitted and cut into quarters lengthwise

2 tablespoons extra-virgin olive oil

2 teaspoons balsamic vinegar

freshly ground black pepper, to taste

SERVES 2

Preheat the oven to 325°F. Place the onion wedges on a baking tray or sheet. Drizzle with a little olive oil. Roast in the oven for 10 minutes. Alternatively, quickly sauté in a hot frying pan or skillet with a little olive oil until the onion just starts to lose its color, but remains firm. Set aside.

Rub the zucchini with a little olive oil. Quickly sear on both sides in a hot frying pan or skillet. If you have a barbecue, sear the zucchini over the bars to give a criss-cross effect. Set aside.

Place the mixed salad leaves in the center of a flat serving plate, reserving some leaves for garnish. Cut the zucchini and roast red bell pepper into 1½-inch lengths. Place the zucchini, red bell pepper, onion, and artichokes around the leaves. Add the sun-dried tomatoes and feta cheese. Sprinkle the olives over the top.

Spoon the olive oil and balsamic vinegar over the top of the salad. Garnish with the reserved mixed leaves and season with black pepper.

Vine-ripened Tomatoes with Goat Cheese & Basil

~~~

TRY TO PURCHASE THE BEST-QUALITY TOMATOES YOU CAN FOR THIS SALAD,
WHETHER THEY BE VINE-RIPENED OR, BETTER STILL, ORGANICALLY GROWN.
CHOOSE BRIGHTLY COLORED FRUIT WITH FIRM FLESH. THE GOAT CHEESE
CAN BE REPLACED WITH FETA OR BOCCONCINI CHEESE, DEPENDING ON YOUR
TASTE. YOU MAY ALSO LIKE TO ADD SUN-DRIED TOMATOES TO THIS SALAD.

2 vine-ripened or organic tomatoes
3 ounces goat cheese, sliced
6 yellow pear tomatoes, halved
½ bunch of basil, sliced into very thin
   strips (or chiffonade as it is known in
   restaurants)
5 teaspoons extra-virgin olive oil
freshly ground black pepper, to taste

SERVES 1–2

Wash the vine-ripened tomatoes very carefully and pat dry. Using a very sharp knife, slice into rounds ¼ inch thick. Lay the tomato slices in a circle on a serving plate. Lay the slices of goat cheese in between the slices of tomato, giving you a layered effect. Place the halves of pear tomato around the outside of the serving plate. Sprinkle the basil strips over the top of the salad and drizzle with the olive oil. Season with the black pepper.

Forest Mushrooms & Spinach with Lemon Thyme & Hazelnuts

〜〜〜

THIS IS A WARM SALAD AND SHOULD ONLY BE PREPARED JUST BEFORE
SERVING. THE TYPE OF MUSHROOMS YOU USE IS ENTIRELY UP TO YOU,
BUT TRY SOMETHING A LITTLE EXOTIC SUCH AS SHIMEJI,
SWISS BROWN, ENOKI, OR SLIPPERY JACK MUSHROOMS.

2 teaspoons walnut oil or olive oil

1 ounce prosciutto or bacon slices, cut into strips about 1¼ inches long

8 ounces assorted mushrooms, washed and sliced into thick pieces

1–2 bunches of baby spinach, stems discarded, rinsed and dried

a few sprigs of lemon thyme

salt and freshly ground black pepper, to taste

4 teaspoons coarsely chopped hazelnuts

SERVES 2

Heat the walnut oil in a small frying pan or skillet over a moderate heat. Add the prosciutto or bacon. Sauté gently until it starts to become golden. Add the mushrooms and sauté quickly.

While the mushrooms are cooking, arrange the spinach leaves in a pile on a serving plate. Add the lemon thyme to the mushroom mixture. Season with salt and pepper. Remove the mushroom mixture from the pan and spoon directly onto the spinach. Drizzle a couple of spoonfuls of the juice from the pan over the salad. Garnish with the hazelnuts and serve immediately.

Mixed Leaf Salad with Baby Tomatoes & Balsamic Vinegar

~~~

A SIMPLE MIXED SALAD INCORPORATING BABY SALAD LEAVES AND ASSORTED VEGETABLES. THE BALSAMIC DRESSING WILL LAST FOR SOME TIME IF STORED IN AN AIRTIGHT CONTAINER IN THE REFRIGERATOR.

BALSAMIC DRESSING
1 teaspoon Dijon mustard
¼ cup balsamic vinegar
½ cup peanut oil
¼ cup olive oil

SALAD
16 cherry tomatoes
16 yellow pear tomatoes
¼ small cucumber, peeled
7 ounces assorted mixed baby salad leaves
 or mesclun, rinsed and dried
handful of bean sprouts
½ handful of snow pea shoots
freshly chopped chives, to garnish

SERVES 4

BALSAMIC DRESSING
Mix the Dijon mustard and balsamic vinegar together in a bowl. Combine the peanut and olive oils. Whisk the mustard and balsamic vinegar mixture. Slowly add the oil to the mixture in a steady stream, whisking continuously, until all the oil is incorporated. Set aside until ready to use.

Slice the cherry and pear tomatoes in half only if necessary (depending on their size). Slice the cucumber in half lengthways and cut into slices. Place the mixed leaves, cucumber slices, tomatoes, bean sprouts, and snow pea shoots in a bowl. Spoon over some of the dressing, just enough to moisten the leaves. Toss the salad using a pair of tongs. Transfer the salad to a serving bowl and garnish with the chives.

Mushrooms with Buttermilk Ranch-style Dressing

~~~~

A HEALTHFUL SALAD WHERE THE MUSHROOMS RETAIN ALL THEIR
NUTRITIONAL GOODNESS. EVEN THOUGH THEY ARE SERVED WITH
A CREAMY DRESSING, IT IS DELICIOUSLY LOW IN FAT.

¼ cup buttermilk

2 ounces fromage blanc

1 teaspoon lemon juice

1 small clove garlic, peeled, blanched in
   boiling water for 1 minute and finely
   chopped

4 teaspoons chopped parsley

4 teaspoons chopped basil

pinch of cayenne (red) pepper

4 ounces mushrooms, washed and thinly
   sliced

1 tomato, sliced

freshly ground black pepper, to taste

freshly chopped chives, to garnish

SERVES 2

Combine the buttermilk, fromage blanc, lemon juice, garlic, parsley, and basil in an electric blender or food processor. Blend or process until smooth. Add the cayenne pepper. Place the mushrooms in a bowl and pour the dressing over the top. Cover and leave to marinate for 30 minutes.

Place the tomato slices around the edge of a serving plate. Spoon the mushroom mixture into the middle. Season with the black pepper. Serve immediately, garnished with the chives.

Roast Pumpkin & Zucchini Salad with Rosemary Aïoli

~~~

A ROAST VEGETABLE SALAD FLAVORED WITH A GARLIC MAYONNAISE AND TOPPED WITH TOASTED SUNFLOWER SEEDS. ANY LEFTOVER MAYONNAISE WILL LAST FOR AT LEAST 3 WEEKS IF STORED IN AN AIRTIGHT CONTAINER IN THE REFRIGERATOR. WHEN MAKING MAYONNAISE, IT IS VERY DIFFICULT TO MAKE QUANTITIES SMALLER THAN THOSE GIVEN BELOW AS THE BASE WILL NOT HAVE SUFFICIENT VOLUME TO INCORPORATE SUCCESSFULLY WITH THE OIL.

ROSEMARY AÏOLI

3 egg yolks
1 tablespoon Dijon mustard
2 teaspoons white wine vinegar
2 cups vegetable oil
2–3 cloves garlic, peeled, blanched in boiling water for 1 minute and finely chopped
½ teaspoon chopped rosemary
salt and freshly ground pepper, to taste

SALAD

¼ pumpkin, cut into wedges about 1¼ inches wide
1 eggplant, cut into slices 1 inch thick
a little olive oil
2 zucchini, halved lengthwise and cut into 1¼-inch pieces

1 red bell pepper, roasted, peeled, seeded, and cut into strips lengthways (see page 12)
salt and freshly ground black pepper, to taste
3 tablespoons sunflower seeds, toasted

SERVES 2

ROSEMARY AÏOLI

Combine the egg yolks, mustard, and vinegar in an electric blender or food processor. With the motor still running, slowly add the oil in a thin stream until it is all incorporated. To thin out, simply add a few drops of hot water. You now have a basic mayonnaise.

Take 1 cup of the mayonnaise and return to the electric blender or food processor. Add the garlic and rosemary. Pulse to blend through the mayonnaise. Set aside until ready to use. Store the leftover mayonnaise in an airtight container in the refrigerator.

Preheat the oven to 350°F. Place the pumpkin wedges in a lightly oiled roasting pan. Place the eggplant slices in a separate lightly oiled roasting pan. Cover with baking parchment. Roast both the pumpkin and the eggplant in the oven for 10–12 minutes, or until cooked. Meanwhile, heat a little olive oil in a frying pan or skillet. Sauté the zucchini for 3 minutes or so. Remove from the pan while still slightly undercooked and firm.

Remove the skin from the pumpkin and cut the flesh into chunks. Place the pumpkin, eggplant, zucchini, and red bell pepper in a salad bowl.

Add ¼ cup Rosemary Aïoli (thin with a little hot water if necessary) to the salad. Season with salt and pepper. Toss the vegetables to coat with the dressing. Sprinkle the sunflower seeds over the top and serve immediately.

Mesclun with Creamy Blue Cheese Dressing

~~~~~

THIS SALAD HAS A VERY CREAMY DRESSING THAT CONTAINS WALNUT OIL.
IF YOU FIND THE WALNUT FLAVOR TOO DOMINANT, SIMPLY REPLACE THE
WALNUT OIL WITH A VEGETABLE ONE. BE CONSERVATIVE WHEN USING THIS
DRESSING; YOU ONLY NEED TO MOISTEN THE SALAD, NOT DROWN IT.

BLUE CHEESE DRESSING

1 egg yolk
1 teaspoon Dijon mustard
2 tablespoons white wine vinegar
⅔ cup walnut oil
3 ounces blue cheese

SALAD

7 ounces mixed salad leaves or mesclun
4 ounces blue cheese, or to taste, diced
12 cherry tomatoes
½ handful of snow pea shoots
freshly ground black pepper, to taste

SERVES 2

BLUE CHEESE DRESSING

Combine the egg yolk, Dijon mustard, and vinegar in an electric blender or food processor. With the motor still running, slowly add the walnut oil so that an emulsion forms. Once all the oil is incorporated, crumble the cheese into the dressing. Blend or process for a few seconds until smooth.

Any leftover dressing will last for up to 2 weeks if stored in an airtight container in the refrigerator.

Combine the salad leaves, blue cheese, cherry tomatoes, and snow pea shoots in a bowl. Add half of the dressing and toss through using a pair of tongs. Season with the black pepper. Add more dressing only if necessary to moisten the leaves.

Salade Niçoise

~

A VARIATION OF THE CLASSIC SALADE NIÇOISE. THIS SALAD IS EXCELLENT WHEN TOMATOES AND GREEN BEANS ARE IN SEASON.

13 ounces green beans, rinsed
8 cherry tomatoes, halved
1 egg, hardboiled and sliced
3 ounces feta cheese, diced
8 kalamata olives, pitted and cut into
    quarters
freshly ground black pepper, to taste
4 teaspoons extra-virgin olive oil
juice of 1 lemon

SERVES 4

Trim the ends of the beans. Steam or boil until just tender, 4–8 minutes depending on the size of the beans. Quickly drain and plunge the beans into a bowl of icy cold water to stop them cooking any further. Remove from the water as soon as they are cold and cut into $1\frac{1}{4}$-inch pieces.

Place the beans, tomatoes, egg, feta cheese, and olives in a salad bowl. Season with the black pepper. Add the olive oil and lemon juice. Toss through the salad and serve.

Just
DESSERTS

AS STRANGE AS IT MAY SEEM, WE HAVE CREATED A RANGE
OF DELICIOUS AND VARIED DESSERT PIZZAS . . . AND, YES,
THE SAUCE AND CHEESE HAVE BEEN REMOVED. AS WITH
SAVORY PIZZAS, THE ONLY LIMITS TO THE ENDLESS
COMBINATIONS POSSIBLE ARE YOUR IMAGINATION
AND CREATIVITY. NOT ALL OF YOUR CREATIONS WILL
NECESSARILY BECOME GASTRONOMIC DELIGHTS,
BUT THE JOY WILL BE IN THE EXPERIMENTING.

THE DESSERT PIZZAS IN THIS CHAPTER ARE A SMALLER
SIZE THAN THE REGULAR OR MEDIUM PIZZAS THROUGHOUT
THE REST OF THE BOOK, WITH THEIR BASES MEASURING
6 INCHES RATHER THAN THE NORMAL 10 INCHES. IF YOU
WISH TO MAKE A LARGE DESSERT PIZZA, SIMPLY USE
THE STANDARD 8-OUNCE BALL OF DOUGH AND
ADJUST YOUR INGREDIENTS ACCORDINGLY.

Crème Pâtissière

~

FOR MOST OF THE FOLLOWING DESSERT PIZZAS, YOU WILL FIRST NEED
TO MAKE A CRÈME PÂTISSIÈRE OR PASTRY CREAM. THE RECIPE IS A
STRAIGHTFORWARD ONE AND THE CRÈME PÂTISSIÈRE WILL LAST FOR UP TO
ONE WEEK IF STORED IN A SEALED CONTAINER IN THE REFRIGERATOR.

2 cups milk
½ teaspoon pure vanilla extract
4 egg yolks
½ cup granulated sugar
½ cup all-purpose flour, sifted
a little confectioners' sugar

MAKES ABOUT 2½ CUPS

Put the milk and vanilla in a medium saucepan. Bring to the boil over a moderate heat. Be careful not to let it scorch.

Place the egg yolks and granulated sugar in a bowl. Whisk together until pale and creamy. Add the flour and mix thoroughly. Pour the hot milk into the mixture and whisk thoroughly.

Return the mixture to the pan and bring to the boil, stirring continuously. Reduce the heat to low and simmer for 2 minutes. The mixture should now be nice and thick.

Transfer to a clean bowl and sprinkle the surface with a little confectioners' sugar. This helps to prevent a skin forming on the top of the crème pâtissière. Allow to cool. If the crème pâtissière is too thick to spread easily, thin with a little light whipping cream before using.

Poached Pear & Hazelnut

THE HINT OF LEMON INFUSED THROUGH THE SUGAR SYRUP GIVES THIS
PIZZA A SUBTLE BALANCE OF SWEET AND SOUR. IT IS PARTICULARLY GOOD
AS AN AFTER-DINNER PIZZA SERVED WITH A STRONG COFFEE OR TWO.

SUGAR SYRUP
1¾ cups granulated sugar
2 cups water
juice of 1 lemon
2–3 slices lemon

PIZZA
4 medium pears (such as Packham)
2 (3-ounce) dough balls (see page 8)
5 teaspoons crème pâtissière (see page 121)
⅓ cup chopped hazelnuts
whipped cream, to serve

MAKES 2 SMALL PIZZAS

SUGAR SYRUP
Combine the sugar, water, lemon juice, and
lemon slices in a medium saucepan. Bring
to the boil and use as required. The cooled
syrup will last indefinitely if stored in an airtight container in the refrigerator.

Peel the pears and slice into quarters lengthwise. Remove the cores. Place in a medium
saucepan and barely cover with hot sugar
syrup. Place a sheet of wax paper on top of
the pears. Cover with a lid or plate so that
the fruit remains submerged. Bring the syrup
almost to the boil. Reduce the heat to a simmer and allow pears to poach until almost
soft. Remove from the heat and allow to cool
in the syrup. When cool, cut the quarters
into slices lengthwise. Set aside.

Place two pizza stones or tiles in the
oven. Heat the oven to 500°F. Roll out the
pizza dough, as described on page 10, so
that you have two bases.

Cover the bases with the crème pâtissière,
keeping a 1-inch border around the edge of
the dough clean.

Lay the pear slices on the bases, starting
with a circle of overlapping pieces around
the edge of the crème pâtissière. Fill the
middle of each base with the remaining
slices. Sprinkle the hazelnuts over the top.

Using a wide spatula or pizza paddle,
gently slide each pizza onto a stone or tile.
Cook for 10 minutes. Remove the pizzas
from the oven when cooked and golden.
Slice each pizza into four pieces using a
large chopping or cook's knife. Serve immediately, accompanied by the whipped
cream.

Apricot & Almond

~~~

APRICOTS, TOASTED ALMONDS, AND DATES, LIBERALLY SPLASHED WITH
AMARETTO, CREATE A MEDLEY FIT FOR ANY OCCASION. THIS PIZZA IS
ESPECIALLY GOOD WITH ICED TEA, ALCOHOLIC OR NON-ALCOHOLIC!

7 ounces dried apricots
hot sugar syrup, to cover (see page 122)
2 (3-ounce) dough balls (see page 8)
5 teaspoons crème pâtissière (see page 121)
2 dates, pitted and cut into quarters
3 tablespoons sliced almonds
2 teaspoons Amaretto (optional)
whipped cream, to serve

MAKES 2 SMALL PIZZAS

Put the dried apricots in a shallow pan. Barely cover with the hot sugar syrup. Place a sheet of wax paper on top of the apricots. Cover with a lid or plate so that the fruit remains submerged. Allow to cool. Strain off any syrup and set the apricots aside.

Place two pizza stones or tiles in the oven. Heat the oven to 500°F. Roll out the pizza dough, as described on page 10, so that you have two bases.

Cover the bases with the crème pâtissière, keeping a 1-inch border around the edge of the dough clean. Lay the apricot halves on the bases, starting with a circle of overlapping pieces around the edge of the crème pâtissière. Fill the middle of each base with the remaining pieces. Place the date pieces on the bases, one on each quarter. Sprinkle the almonds over the top. Drizzle with the Amaretto (if using).

Using a wide spatula or pizza paddle, gently slide each pizza onto a stone or tile. Cook for 10 minutes. Remove from the oven when cooked and golden. Slice each pizza into four pieces using a large chopping or cook's knife. Serve immediately, accompanied by the whipped cream.

Banana & Passion Fruit

~~~

ANOTHER EXAMPLE OF CLASSIC FLAVORS COMBINING TO CREATE
GASTRONOMIC HARMONY. AN ABSOLUTELY LUSCIOUS PIZZA,
GUARANTEED TO KEEP THEM COMING BACK FOR MORE.

2 (3-ounce) dough balls (see page 8)
5 teaspoons crème pâtissière (see page 121)
1 large banana or 2 medium bananas
2–3 tablespoons passion fruit pulp
¼ cup roughly chopped pistachio nuts
whipped cream, to serve

MAKES 2 SMALL PIZZAS

Place two pizza stones or tiles in the oven. Heat the oven to 500°F. Roll out the pizza dough, as described on page 10, so that you have two bases.

Cover the bases with the crème pâtissière, keeping a 1-inch border around the edge of the dough clean.

Slice the banana on a 45-degree angle so that you have nice, long pieces. Lay the banana on the bases, starting with a circle of overlapping pieces around the edge of the crème pâtissière. Fill the middle of each base with the remaining pieces. Spoon over the passionfruit pulp and sprinkle the pistachios over the top.

Using a wide spatula or pizza paddle, gently slide each pizza onto a stone or tile. Cook for 10 minutes. Remove from the oven when cooked and golden. Slice each pizza into four pieces using a large chopping or cook's knife. Serve immediately, accompanied by the whipped cream.

Wild Raspberry & Coconut

~~~

FROM TIME TO TIME I USE NATIVE RASPBERRIES FOR THIS PIZZA. THESE ARE
CLOSER IN SHAPE TO THE STRAWBERRY AND HAVE MORE SEEDS THAN
THE COMMON RASPBERRY. YOU MAY BE ABLE TO FIND NATIVE RASPBERRIES
IN THE FROZEN FOOD SECTION OF A VERY WELL-STOCKED DELICATESSEN.

2 pints raspberries
hot sugar syrup, to cover (see page 122)
2 (3-ounce) dough balls (see page 8)
5 teaspoons crème pâtissière (see page 121)
3 egg whites
½ cup granulated sugar
3 cups shredded coconut
whipped cream or rich vanilla ice cream,
   to serve

MAKES 2 SMALL PIZZAS

Put the raspberries in a shallow pan. Barely
cover with the hot sugar syrup. Place a sheet
of wax paper on top of the raspberries.
Cover with a lid or plate so that the fruit
remains submerged. Allow to cool. Strain
off any syrup and set the raspberries aside.

Place two pizza stones or tiles in the
oven. Heat the oven to 500°F. Roll out the
pizza dough, as described on page 10, so
that you have two bases.

Cover the bases with the crème pâtissière,
keeping a 1-inch border around the edge of
the dough clean. Using a spoon, place the
raspberries on the bases. Use enough raspberries to make a plentiful topping.

Whisk the egg whites in an electric
mixer until firm. Add the sugar gradually,
whisking continuously, and then the coconut.
You should have a nice thick paste. Place a
thin layer of coconut mixture on top of the
raspberries.

Using a wide spatula or pizza paddle,
gently slide each pizza onto a stone or tile.
Cook for 10 minutes. Remove the pizzas
from the oven when cooked and golden.
Slice each pizza into four pieces using a
large chopping or cook's knife. Serve immediately, accompanied by the whipped cream
or vanilla ice cream.

Granny Smith Apple Crumble

~~~

THIS PIZZA IS A VARIATION ON TRADITIONAL APPLE CRUMBLE, ONE OF THOSE OLD-FASHIONED RECIPES THAT IS A DEFINITE WINTER FAVORITE. GRANNY SMITH APPLES ARE DELICIOUS COOKING APPLES, WITH THEIR SLIGHTLY TART FLAVOR, AND ARE PERFECT FOR THIS RECIPE. THIS PIZZA, LIKE ITS INSPIRATION, TASTES EVEN BETTER WHEN SERVED WITH A GENEROUS DOLLOP OF CINNAMON ICE CREAM.

CRUMBLE TOPPING
1¼ cups whole wheat flour
⅔ cup unsalted butter
⅓ cup brown sugar
⅓ cup sliced almonds
3 tablespoons wheat germ
3 tablespoons rolled oats

CRUMBLE
2 large Granny Smith apples
a little sugar
pinch of ground cinnamon
2 (3-ounce) dough balls (see page 8)
5 teaspoons crème pâtissière (see page 121)
1 tablespoon currants
whipped cream or cinnamon ice cream,
  to serve

MAKES 2 SMALL PIZZAS

CRUMBLE TOPPING
Put the flour in a bowl. Rub the butter into the flour until the mixture resembles fine breadcrumbs. Add the brown sugar, almonds, wheat germ, and rolled oats. Mix thoroughly and set aside.

Peel and quarter the apples lengthways. Remove the cores and slice into strips lengthways. Place the apples in a frying pan or skillet with a little sugar and the cinnamon. Cook gently over a medium heat until the sugar dissolves and the apple has softened slightly. Remove from the heat and allow to cool.

Place two pizza stones or tiles in the oven. Heat the oven to 500°F. Roll out the pizza dough, as described on page 10, so that you have two bases. Cover the bases with the crème pâtissière, keeping a 1-inch border around the edge of the dough clean.

Lay the apple slices on the bases, starting with a circle of overlapping pieces around the edge of the crème pâtissière. Fill the middle of each base with the remaining apple, continuing in the same circular pattern. Add the currants. Sprinkle the crumble mixture over the top.

Using a wide spatula or pizza paddle, gently slide each pizza onto a stone or tile. Cook for 10 minutes. Remove the pizzas from the oven when cooked and golden. Slice each pizza into four pieces using a large chopping or cook's knife. Serve immediately, accompanied by the whipped cream or cinnamon ice cream.

Macadamia, Pecan, & Orange

〜

IN THIS RECIPE, THE DOUGH IS USED TO LINE A PIE DISH RATHER
THAN BEING BAKED FLAT. MAKE SURE THAT YOU CUT THE DOUGH OUT
SLIGHTLY LARGER THAN THE DISH, AS IT WILL SHRINK AS IT BAKES.

2 (3-ounce) dough balls (see page 8)
4 eggs
⅔ cup granulated sugar
1 cup light corn syrup
1 teaspoon pure vanilla extract
½ cup macadamia nuts, roughly chopped
⅔ cup pecans, roughly chopped
3 blood or other oranges, peeled and pith
  removed, cut into slices
whipped cream, to serve

MAKES 2 SMALL PIES

Preheat the oven to 300°F. Roll out the pizza dough, as described on page 10, so that you have two rounds of dough. Lightly grease two 4- to 5-inch pie pans. Line each pan with a round of dough. Prick the dough all over with a fork and then cover with baking parchment. Fill each pie shell with baking beans or rice. Bake in the oven for 12 minutes or until the dough is cooked on the bottom. The pie shells are now ready to use. Increase the oven temperature to 350°F.

Combine the eggs and sugar in a bowl. Whisk thoroughly. Slowly add the corn syrup and vanilla essence, whisking as you do so. Add the macadamia nuts and pecans. Combine thoroughly. Pour this mixture into the pie shells and bake for 35 minutes, or until set. Remove from the oven and allow to cool.

Lay the sliced oranges on the top of each pie in a circular pattern, slightly overlapping each slice. Slice each pie into four pieces using a large chopping or cook's knife. Serve immediately, accompanied by the whipped cream.

Mango & Pink Peppercorn

A HOT AND SWEET COMBINATION, WITH THE FIERY PEPPERCORNS
KEEPING THE SWEETNESS OF THE MANGO IN BALANCE.
A TOUCH OF FRESH MINT ROUNDS OUT THE FLAVOR.

2 (3-ounce) dough balls (see page 8)
5 teaspoons crème pâtissière (see page 121)
2 mangoes, peeled and sliced
½ cup puréed mango slices
3–4 tablespoons water
4 teaspoons pink peppercorns (available in good delicatessens or gourmet stores)
4–5 mint leaves, finely chopped
whipped cream, to serve

MAKES 2 SMALL PIZZAS

Place two pizza stones or tiles in the oven. Heat the oven to 500°F. Roll out the pizza dough, as described on page 10, so that you have two bases. Cover the bases with the crème pâtissière, keeping a 1-inch border around the edge of the dough clean.

Place the sliced mango on top of the crème pâtissière, layering it from the border inwards. Put the mango purée into a small saucepan. Add enough water to make a thick sauce consistency. Add the pink peppercorns and bring the mixture to the boil. Remove from the heat and add the mint. Mix thoroughly. Spoon the sauce over the mango slices, keeping the edge of the dough clean.

Using a wide spatula or pizza paddle, gently slide each pizza onto a stone or tile. Cook for 10 minutes. Remove the pizzas from the oven when cooked and golden. Slice each pizza into four pieces using a large chopping or cook's knife. Serve immediately, accompanied by the whipped cream.

Mango, Ginger, & Lime

~~~~

A TROPICAL BLEND OF MANGO AND LIME, WITH THE GINGER
ADDING A TOUCH OF ORIENTAL FLAVOR. THIS PIZZA PROVIDES
A NOT-SO-SWEET DESSERT ALTERNATIVE.

2 limes
sugar syrup, to cover (see page 122)
2 (3-ounce) dough balls (see page 8)
5 teaspoons crème pâtissière (see page 121)
2 mangoes, peeled and sliced
small piece of ginger, peeled and finely
  grated
whipped cream, to serve

MAKES 2 SMALL PIZZAS

Remove the peel from the limes with a peeler or with a sharp knife. Slice the peel into very thin strips. Reserve the lime flesh for another use. Blanch the peel in fresh boiling water 5 times before using. This opens the pores of the peel, removing the bitter acids and allowing the sugar to penetrate. Place the peel in a small saucepan and cover with sugar syrup. Bring to the boil and simmer gently until the peel starts to become transparent, 30–40 minutes depending on the thickness of the peel. Allow the candied lime to cool in the syrup.

Place two pizza stones or tiles in the oven. Heat the oven to 500°F. Roll out the pizza dough, as described on page 10, so that you have two bases. Cover the bases with the crème pâtissière, keeping a 1-inch border around the edge of the dough clean.

Place the sliced mango on top of the crème pâtissière, layering it from the border inwards. Sprinkle the ginger over the mango, in moderation. Take some strips of candied lime and place on top of the ginger (it does not matter if some of the syrup goes onto the pizzas as well).

Using a wide spatula or pizza paddle, gently slide each pizza onto a stone or tile. Cook for 10 minutes. Remove the pizzas from the oven when cooked and golden. Slice each pizza into four pieces using a large chopping or cook's knife. Serve immediately, accompanied by the whipped cream.

Rhubarb & Apple

~~~

A "COMFORT" PIZZA WHICH REMINDS ME OF EATING RHUBARB IN MY
MOTHER'S KITCHEN WHEN I WAS A CHILD. COVER WITH THE CRUMBLE TOPPING
ON PAGE 126 TO TRANSFORM THIS PIZZA INTO A MEMORABLE DESSERT PIE.

3 stalks rhubarb, peeled and cut into
  2-inch pieces
1 large Granny Smith apple, peeled,
  quartered and chopped into pieces
hot sugar syrup, to cover (see page 122)
pinch of ground cinnamon
2 (3-ounce) dough balls (see page 8)
5 teaspoons crème pâtissière (see page 121)
whipped cream, to serve

MAKES 2 SMALL PIZZAS

Put the rhubarb and apple into a medium saucepan. Cover with the hot sugar syrup and add the cinnamon. Place a sheet of wax paper on top of the apple and rhubarb. Cover with a lid or plate so that the fruit remains submerged. Bring almost to the boil, then reduce the heat to a simmer. Poach gently until the apple has softened. Strain off any syrup and allow the mixture to cool in a strainer. The rhubarb should be broken up through the apple.

Place two pizza stones or tiles in the oven. Heat the oven to 500°F. Roll out the pizza dough, as described on page 10, so that you have two bases. Cover the bases with the crème pâtissière, keeping a 1-inch border around the edge of the dough clean.

Spoon the apple and rhubarb mixture over the crème pâtissière. Use enough mixture to give a plentiful topping.

Using a wide spatula or pizza paddle, gently slide each pizza onto a stone or tile. Cook for 10 minutes. Remove the pizzas from the oven when cooked and golden. Slice each pizza into four pieces using a large chopping or cook's knife. Serve immediately, accompanied by the whipped cream.

Tofu, Banana, & Chocolate

〜〜〜

ONCE AGAIN, THIS RECIPE IS FOR A PIE RATHER THAN A FLAT PIZZA.
DON'T BE PUT OFF BY THE TOFU IN THIS MOUTHWATERING PIE.
ONCE YOU'VE TRIED IT, YOU'LL FIND IT IRRESISTIBLE.

2 (3-ounce) dough balls (see page 8)
7 ounces cottage cheese
7 ounces firm tofu
¼ cup honey
1 banana, mashed
juice of ½ lemon
½ cup all-purpose flour

CHOCOLATE GANACHE

7 ounces semisweet chocolate, roughly
  chopped
⅔ cup light whipped cream

MAKES 2 SMALL PIES

Preheat the oven to 300°F.

Roll out the pizza dough, as described on page 10, so that you have two rounds of dough. Lightly grease two 4- to 5-inch pie pans. Line each pan with a round of dough. Prick the dough all over with a fork and then cover with baking parchment. Fill each pie shell with baking beans or rice. Bake in the oven for 12 minutes, or until the dough is cooked on the bottom. The pie shells are now ready to use.

Increase the oven temperature to 325°F.

Combine the cottage cheese, tofu, honey, banana, and lemon juice in a bowl. Stir in the flour and mix thoroughly. Pour the mixture into the prepared pie shells, leaving ¼ inch at the top for the Chocolate Ganache. Bake in the oven for 20 minutes. Remove from the oven and allow to cool. Meanwhile, make the Chocolate Ganache.

CHOCOLATE GANACHE

Place the chocolate in a ceramic or glass bowl. Pour the cream into a saucepan. Bring almost to the boil.

Add half of the cream to the chocolate and stir until the chocolate is partially melted. Stir in the remaining cream and continue to stir until the chocolate is completely melted and the ganache is smooth.

Spoon over the top of the cooled pies and allow to set before serving.

Calzone of Mixed Berries, Spearmint, & Mascarpone

~~~

A FOLDED PIZZA OF SEASONAL BERRIES WITH MASCARPONE CHEESE MAKES FOR
A DELICIOUS STUFFED PIZZA. THE MASCARPONE MAY SEPARATE SLIGHTLY
WHEN COOKED, BUT THE SUPERB FLAVOR DOES NOT CHANGE AT ALL.

2 (8-ounce) dough balls (see page 8)
8 ounces assorted seasonal berries (such as
  strawberries, raspberries, blueberries,
  or blackberries)
3 ounces mascarpone cheese, softened to
  room temperature
8 spearmint leaves, chopped
2 teaspoons chopped nuts (such as walnuts, hazelnuts, or pistachio nuts)
1 teaspoon shredded coconut
confectioners' sugar, for dusting

MAKES 2 SMALL CALZONES

Place two pizza stones or tiles in the oven.
Heat the oven to 475°F. Calzones require
a slightly lower cooking temperature and a
longer cooking time than ordinary pizzas.

Roll out the pizza dough, as described on
page 10, so that you have two bases. Find
a plate approximately 7 inches in diameter
and place it face down on one of the bases.
Take a sharp knife and run it around the outside of the plate to cut a smaller base.

Remove the plate. You should now have a
round, smooth-edged base. Repeat with the
other base.

Place all the berries in a bowl. Add the
mascarpone cheese, spearmint, nuts, and
coconut. Gently fold the mascarpone through
the mixture.

Brush any excess flour from the dough.
Place half the berry mixture on one half only
of each base. Keep at least a 1-inch border
around the edge of the dough clean. Brush
the border with a few drops of water. Fold
the dough over so that the edges meet. Press
together with a fork, ensuring that the edges
are completely sealed. Once again, brush
any excess flour from the outside of the
dough. Lightly dust the calzones with confectioners' sugar.

Using a wide spatula or pizza paddle,
gently slide each calzone onto a stone or
tile. Cook for 12 minutes. Remove the calzones from the oven when cooked and
golden. Place directly onto serving plates
and slice each calzone in half using a large
chopping or cook's knife. Serve immediately.

Index

~~~